THE TOMBSTONE EXPRESS

ADVENTURES IN POLICE MOTORCYCLE ESCORTS

STEVE EDWARDS

BRILLIANT CROW PUBLISHING

ISBN: 979-8-9853659-0-0

LCCN: 2022903467

Book cover designed by: Milan Jovanovic & Steve Edwards

Printed in the United States of America

1st Edition

DISCLAIMER

My memories of the exact details of these events is not perfect and are provided to the best of my recollection. Nicknames have been used or created to keep the privacy of those they refer to.

There is some profanity in here at times, as I tend to swear a lot, but I cut most of it out.

CONTENTS

 **JULY 11TH, 1996**

I t was a warm night in Tigard, Oregon, as I arrived at my ten year high school reunion on a 500cc Yamaha Virago. I had no interest in going, seeing as how high school was something I was more interested in forgetting than remembering, but my oldest friend had talked me into it. I had good reason for not wanting to see most of these people. Bullies from a decade ago who clearly hadn't matured a day, still held a grudge for never beating the shit out of me like they'd wanted to.

Once inside, people told me I had gained weight, as I if I didn't know and they were conveying breaking news. There was the occasional person I was happy to see that made it all worthwhile, like Kim. She still had a magnetic personality everyone gravitated to. In a small circle of friendly classmates, she asked "So, what do you do for work?"

Dressed in my Levi's and a T shirt, I told the truth.

"I work for an escort service."

Mouths formerly closed were now slightly agape, as they all visually took stock of me from head to toe, checking to see if they had missed something.

"No, seriously" one of them said, "What do you do?"

"I told you. I work for an escort company."

And I just let that hang there for a while.

 **RIDE 1 - 2**

I t was the best job I ever had. By far. I was young, hungry and fearless enough to take on such a gig and see where it would go. To wake up every day to a new adventure was something to get excited about. You never knew what the next day would hold and it was worth shooting up out of bed when the alarm would go off to find out what it would be. I mean really, how often do you feel like that? To spend those days and months getting paid to ride monster cop bikes, have respect and dignity and take pride in what I was doing, was a very rare feeling for me at the time. Despite all the hardships, challenges and stress of those days, I cherish those times and want to share them with you.

But these were not recent days. It was back in the 90's, before the turn of the millennium. That might not seem like much to anyone around my age, but to younger generations, who can't imagine life before the internet, or without taking a smartphone everywhere they go, they were definitely different times. Even I look back on those days as an almost dark age compared to what we take for granted now. So let me paint a picture for you of the struggles and joys and challenges of that medieval age, the details of which are clear to me only because after every ride, I came home and wrote about the day's experiences for hours while they were still fresh in my mind. Without having done that, this book would be a short summary of hazy memories and vague recollections.

It was April of 1996 in Portland, Oregon. I was a few months shy of turning 28 years old, and as far as I was concerned, my life was in the crapper. I was underemployed; my college student loans, which I couldn't pay a dime towards, were in danger of going to default and being sent to any number of overzealous collection agencies, with the prospect of having my wages garnished, providing I ever had wages to earn in the future. I frequently had to 'borrow' money from parents just to pay the rent. 'Borrow' in the sense that if I ever became rich, which was less likely than getting hit by an asteroid, I could pay them back. I was so poor, I didn't have a car, just that sputtering crappy Yamaha Virago that constantly had starting problems because the previous owner had messed with the electrical wiring and screwed it all up, but it was a big step up from 7 years of riding local buses. They were hard, hard times.

I was a constant mix of emotions; frustrated, depressed, angry, despondent, consumed with loneliness, a sense of being lost, a confirmed underachiever, my life was stuck in a rut and I needed to get out of it. That was all about to change.

I hadn't had any construction work for two months with my brother in law's construction company, where I was a flagger, one of those nameless faceless bozos holding an orange and red stop and slow sign that every car driver hates to see. I had exhausted my search of the local temp agencies and the phone wasn't ringing. Apparently someone whose greatest skill set was filmmaking wasn't in great demand. Employers wanted some-thing more… practical. Again, recall this is in the 90's, when the internet was just beginning to take off. Websites we now take for granted didn't even exist. If you want to find a job in the 21st century, the first thing you do is jump online and sift through the many recruiting or job posting and social media sites you have readily available at your fingertips 24/7. If you wanted to find a job back then, there were basically two options, having connections, which I didn't have, or checking the print newspaper want ads. The Sunday edition of The Oregonian was my best hope. It posted the most job ads you could find in the Portland area, and if you didn't see a job there for you then, you were screwed for a week. Another week of hand wringing and worry, no interviews, no income and expenses mounting. That's just the way it was.

So one such Sunday, as I was looking through the paper, for plumbers, electricians and jobs with skill sets I just didn't have, two small lines that seemed to drown in the sea of print jumped out at me. It read, 'Experienced motorcycle riders needed for funeral procession escorts', or something to that effect. I couldn't believe it, the ad might as well have been listed under section 420: 'Jobs for Steve Edwards, that Steve Edwards could actually get'. It seemed too good to be true. The key word in the ad that gave me pause was Experienced. I had only been riding a motorcycle for around a year after taking a community college class to get my riding license. I was the furthest thing from what you would call seasoned.

When I called the company and talked to a guy known as Hollywood, the president, I found out it was even better than I thought. They train you to ride a 1000cc cop Kawasaki, a classic police model for years, as seen in Terminator 2 and lots of other movies of the time. It was the kind of bike I actually thought about getting as my first, but was way out of my price range.

I went out to the company offices and filled out the application and had an interview with the pres a couple days later. Talk about chance luck, Hollywood and I talked about film-making for the first twenty minutes. He had just got back from L.A., working on a mini series where he was a second unit director, 2nd assistant director or something like that. He was getting psyched about directing his first big film that was going to be about rogue stuntmen pulling off a bank robbery. He'd been a Hollywood stuntman for a number of years, playing everything from Jason of Friday the 13th movies, the killer with the hockey mask, to jumping motorcycles over rotating heli-copter blades. He mentioned a writer friend he'd been working with and was obviously well connected. He and many of his friends were clearly inside the industry, unlike me, who was so far outside the industry I couldn't throw rocks at it.

On top of him being the president of the company and a professional stuntman, he was also an active Portland police officer. When he rode, he rode with his gun.

I mentioned my screenplay that I had spent years writing, which I had just sent off to a producer, but we got on with the interview because the clock was ticking. The fact that I was an O.D.O.T. certified flagger with experience in traffic control, as well as had a clean driving record, (only because I had nothing to drive for three years) probably helped my cause. What was not in my favor was the fact that I'd only been riding a motor-cycle for a year at that point. Their policy was not to hire people with less than two years riding experience, and not to take people who only ride in summer because they're panzies. So, my motto was 'Appear Trainable'.

Of all the people that inquired and they interviewed, around 100 I was told, they chose three of us. I was honored. I felt like an astronaut that appeared to have the right stuff. Now it was up to me to prove they hadn't made the wrong choice. Soon afterwards, they had the three of us new recruits meet at an unused parking lot on a dry Sunday morning. They wanted to see what we already knew, how well we got a feel for the bikes, or if we couldn't cut it all. There was Hollywood and two other motorcycle cops to critique and advise us on our performances.

Those cop Kawasakis are a barge on wheels. They're about 500 pounds dry weight, a lot of bike to handle. As if that weren't enough, they rode about six inches higher than my bike, which meant I was standing on my tip toes when I touched the ground, never could get my feet flat on the pavement. It put me at a real disadvantage at first. The bikes were utterly daunting. On my own, far lighter bike, it could never tip over when stopped. It was always light enough to keep from falling. The same wasn't true with me and those cop bikes.

They had us ride in a straight line, slow to a stop and make a tight turn. We would do this for left and right, this way and that. It was super simple stuff that all of us could do with our eyes closed on our own bikes, but to try and muscle these huge machines around was exposing all of our biggest weaknesses real fast. Even the near-expert new guy was doing his braking wrong, and that was a bad habit they were going to have to break him of. My problem was keeping the bike balanced when at a stop. I was safest and doing things right when I was moving, but when I had to put my foot on the ground, then go into a super tight turn, it would get slow enough that I would lose my inertia and the bike would fall into the turn. Wrongfully, I fought to keep it up and it nearly threw me off because it goes down so hard.

I thought I blew it, like it was all over right there. They showed me the correct way to get the bike back up because I was going about it all wrong. Standing it back up, it looked like I had cracked the front fender, but they told me it was already there, to get back on the bike and not to worry about it. They've all done it too.

The other guy in training couldn't help but laugh and say, "Glad it was you and not me."

The three guys that trained us all had nicknames, given to each other during their breaking in days over a decade ago. Handyman, Kickstand, Snapshot, Hollywood, and so on. There's a reason to every nickname, just like most Native Americans in Sacagawea's time, something memorable about them or something happens and the name sticks. Here I was in my breaking-in days and I was afraid I was going to get a nickname I couldn't stand, something right out of the movie Animal House, like Flounder. "Hey Flounder, come on, we're waiting on ya!" To my surprise, despite being the weakest and least experienced rider, they kept me on.

They had the three of us come in for some instruction on how to deal with intersections and traffic, just to give us an idea of what to expect. We were given a phone number for a recorded message to call every night around six to get instructions for the next days' rides. Hollywood told us that the garage where everything was kept had been plagued for years by strange events and unexplainable occurrences. It's as if he were telling us it were haunted in not so many words. The occurrences he mentioned didn't strike me as something spiritual effecting the physical world, more so as 'shit happens', especially when you've got a practical joker in your employ.

A week went by without any progress. No rides or anything. I wanted to get more familiar with the bike and ride it around the blocks near the garage before riding in a procession. All I had done so far was ride it in a parking lot and tipped it over.

The weather had been dry and stable the whole week. Sunday, Mother's Day of '96, the weather went to shit. I rode a half hour home from my sisters' place in Tualatin in a downpour. That's what the weather was supposed to be like all the next week. When I got home I found out I was going to be in not one, but two processions the next day. Needless to say, I was nervous. Expert riders who had done these things for years for this company had been injured, burned and even killed in this line of work. It wasn't inconceivable that I could do something that would put me in a tough spot, in the hospital, or in the ground.

I had all of my uniform except for the pants. It was enough to ride. Because I got the job, I had to get a black leather coat, and cheap. I didn't have the money to spend on something expensive like that, and good leather ain't cheap. I called around to some second hand stores and found Ace's 10 to 10, which had a dozen black leather coats all under a hundred bucks. I'd been unemployed for months and didn't have enough to even to pay the rent.

I cashed my federal tax refund, (the first time I'd ever got one) and went to Ace's. When I walked in there, some old guy was standing at the counter zapping a stun gun in the air. He was a 50 to 60 year old guy waving this thing around at the store owner and some teenage runt like he was an imma-ture gradeschool kid showing off his new, dangerous toy. Its arc of electricity flashing between those two poles is about as threatening as it gets. When he waved it near me, as if to make me jumpy, I made it clear I didn't share his sense of humor.

Of the ten black leather coats, there was one that was the clear standout. It was thick leather, looked unworn and respectable from a uniform standpoint. No surprise it was the most expensive of them all, 80 bucks. It was a perfect fit, brand new as far as anyone could tell, and exactly what I needed. I had about $200 bucks on me, so I shoved the rest into my right pocket and held up seventy bucks on the counter, wearing the coat.

"I've got to have this coat for a job if you can believe that. I got seventy bucks. Can you pull that off without anyone getting pissed?" -Knowing I'm talking to the owner. He did a real good act of reluctantly taking the money, feeling like I had really made a steal of the coat, which I later found out I had.

I walked out of Ace's feeling awesome. I was so proud of myself for getting that coat for seventy bucks I was high off that for days. I saw the exact same coat on the racks brand new for $200-$250. That was the icing on the cake.

Man, it sucks being poor.

The seven point gold star badge cost the company 47 bucks, saying Special Patrolman, with the official State of Oregon seal. It's what the motorcycle cops wear, the real deal, requiring authorization from certified organizations to get it. You can't just walk into a police uniform store and buy one, you have to be on a list and they're expecting you. Stick this thing on a nice black leather coat, put a cop helmet on him, give him a cop Kawasaki with lights and all, and you've got yourself a look-alike cop. The things I didn't have were a gun and handcuffs.

We filled up with gas at a Texaco station down the street and headed out to the chapel where our first service was in session. I was supposed to share the lane with another cycle, staying parallel to him at all times. I'd never had to do this before and found it a great skill sharpener. Instead of weaving all around the lane like you would on your own bike, using the best part of the lane, imagine riding in a concrete corridor at anywhere from 10 to 60 miles an hour with two feet of room on each side. It really makes you pay attention as you keep reminding yourself that if you really concentrate, you can do it. And I would.

A lot of that job was hurry up and wait. You race to get to the church or funeral home on time (I think it's just because they like going exceptionally fast and they're used to it) and then you wait for what feels like forever for the service to be over so you can get on with the procession, the real job where all the training meets the true test. You want to get it on already.

I had never seen a funeral procession with police escort before and didn't know how it worked. What happens is that someone stops the public traffic on the first turn from the church, and another bike leads the hearse into the street and the long chain of uninterrupted cars, the procession, begins. It's a leaping-frogging deal, where the guy who held the last intersection cruises back up in front of the hearse, and the guy who was just leading the hearse takes off to hold the next intersection, so the procession won't have to come to a stop anywhere along the way and won't get broken up by traffic lights or unwanted cars getting in our line and suddenly doing something unexpected. Imagine three dozen cars driving through a red light against cross traffic because a single motor-cycle cop is in the middle of the intersection having stopped traffic in four directions. That's how it goes when things go smoothly. Things are not always that smooth.

That's how two experienced riders pull off a procession, the leap-frogging deal. But with us three new riders, we would be bumping for a while. Bumping is when the newest rider, a break-in, basically would lead the hearse at a slow speed, so as to have the front row seat in watching how processions are done. And it allows the break-in to be partially involved by pulling up directly behind the rider stopped at a secured inter-section, allowing the experienced rider to take off to secure the next intersection. The break-in, being me, would stay at the intersection until the last car came by and then I'd jam up back to the front in the oncoming traffic lane, or whichever side of the street worked best in getting ahead of the hearse again.

I remember that jamming in the oncoming lane with traffic coming at you was a thrill hard to compare. I can't stand roller coasters or other people's driving because I'm not in control, but I couldn't get enough of this rush. The oncoming cars would either completely pull over and stop when they saw me coming, would make a little room and slow down as they passed, or to spite me, they'd give no room and their feet never let up on the gas.

In the state of Oregon, it's illegal for funeral escorts to use their sirens for any reason during a funeral procession. The only thing we had to get the attention of drivers with was our flashy bikes and blaring whistles, like a traffic cop.

The processions I did that day were typically 10-15 miles an hour below the posted speed limit. That's to try and give enough time for a rider to reach the next intersection and shut it down before the hearse gets there. One of the coolest things about those runs was seeing the guy who stays behind at the intersection say over the radio, "Comin' up on your left."

He comes screaming up behind me, "Vroooom!", at freaking Mach 2 and cuts into my lane not even a car length ahead, screaming up to the red light. It's a rush. It really gets the adrenaline in the blood.

As if that weren't fun enough, the ride to the next funeral was a screaming eagle, tear-assing ride just because those guys love speed. Riding at 70 miles an hour on highways and country backroads is nothing new, but doing it on a 1000 cc cop motorcycle, sharing the lane with another cop bike only two feet away, taking corners and changing lanes in tandem is something altogether different. It's illegal to ride in tandem as a 'civilian' because it's dangerous and takes a good deal of skill and communication, sharing an understood timing. We took the treacherous Terwilliger curves of I-5 at 55 miles and hour, even though the cops have routinely been giving out tickets for cars going anything over 50 through the two accident-prone corners.

.   .   .

WHAT A SENSE of dread overcomes me when I see the sheet of water in the sky that is a downpour looming over us and soaking everything in its path. This was the first time I'd done any riding without my full face helmet and visor, something I was distinctly worried about. Ever since I was eighteen, I'd needed glasses to be able to really see just about anything, reading, t.v., driving, whatever. Now with the rain sheeting both sides of my prescription shades and the water pooling in my eyes, everything was a blur. That and my eyes were watering in the wind.

The guys riding tandem a few car lengths ahead just became four orange lights in the wavy, dark blur. At least I wasn't thirsty anymore. The windshield collected enough water to make it nothing but an obstacle to look around, and lord knows I was too damn short to see over it.

The only thing to do was to lose the glasses and literally lean over to crane my neck to see around the Plexiglas. Scary, scary stuff for me at the time. Or anytime. I was at the total mercy of chance and probability, if something went wrong or unexpected, it would be Pavement Time. A pothole or any junk in the road, someone pulls out in front of me, or sudden, emergency braking, would mean doom for sure. Riding near-blind through a downpour so early on was pretty hairy, but nothing disastrous happened, and I felt lucky I came away soaked but unscathed.

We made it to the cemetery and when I had to pull an extremely tight turn without going into oncoming traffic, I had the same problem as in the parking lot, too tight a turn, lost my inertia and the bike fell to the ground at a dead stop. But the problem was made worse by the fact that I was too short to save it. Once again I foolishly fought to keep it from going over, which would be enough to give somebody a hernia or throw out their back. Handyman told me next time just to let it fall over, it's not worth getting injured trying to keep a bike up that's going over anyway. And I knew there would be a next time.

We hoisted the bike up and got back to the office no problem. I had managed to survive my first couple rides without completely screwing up.

 **RIDE 3**

My next ride came on a Saturday morning at what I considered the crack of dawn. I had set my alarm for 6 a.m. and crashed sometime around one in the morning. The alarm didn't go off or I slept right through it. For some reason, I awoke at 7:45 and shot out of bed like a jolt from the electric chair. I was sweating from freaking out before I could even get my clothes on. My head felt like it was going to explode from the pressure, or that it would implode and crush itself from the vice squeezing at my temples. I put the badge on my leather coat and raced out the door. I screamed 90 blocks up the main street through southeast Portland at least 15 miles an hour over the speed limit, absolutely hell bent. I got to the garage, where they were surprised to see me, thinking I was a no show. The funeral service was already in progress only a mile or so away. I fired up the Kawasaki and tore out of there, the basic pre-ride checks and warm ups out of the question.

I found the church with some circling around the neighborhood in a panic. I joined my fellow riders near the hearse. They too were surprised to see me. They briefly explained the route and the cemetery we were going to. Fortunately, it would be a short ride to River View Cemetery, one that I had a long history with of shooting pictures and researching the rich tales of the founders of Stumptown. The most senior rider on this run was a civilian who'd been given the nickname Jackknife years earlier. I'd rode with him at least once before. As I was passing out breath mints, he commented, "Somebody smells like a brewery."

So we get the procession underway and I'm in a largely observational and helping out role, cruising along, taking it all in. As the lead rider in front of the hearse, bumping, I should have had no problem, but it was a roundabout way to the cemetery through residential neighborhoods and I didn't have a clue where we were going, especially when we pulled into a cul-de-sac that had eight intersecting avenues leading away from it. It was like I was circling the caravan around the Arc De Triomphe and I didn't know which side street they wanted to get off on. It was a toss up for which road to choose, and I guessed wrong. The hearse chose right. I circled back around and took the lead again. Later, I chose another wrong turn, largely because I wasn't in radio contact with the other riders. It was just a bad situation all around.

We made it to the cemetery without any major incidents, just a few minors. On the bright side, I handled the bike with much more skill, rode in tandem formation better, and didn't tip it over, which was a distinct possibility considering my abilities at the time. So, yeah for me, despite myself.

 **RIDE 4**

My fourth ride was on a Friday, a payday, with Hollywood. I had heaped extra pressure on myself not to screw up. We made the ride to Willamette National Cemetery without a hitch, at least, as far as I was concerned. I didn't make any wrong turns, get too far ahead or too close to the hearse following me, and had absolutely no problems with the bike. The weather was perfect. At one point when I was leading the procession past a church, some scruffy little dog saw me and ran into the street to chase me. I tried to wave it away and scare it off by revving the engine, but it just wanted to chase me more. Attack the big beast I guess. I sped up and saw this petty little tyrant in my mirror, cutting into the line of cars in behind the hearse. Thought I was going to hear the sharp squeal of the dog but it never came. It must have just baaaarely been missed by the next car; it's a wonder it didn't cause an accident and stop the whole procession with some unforeseeable dog tragedy.

Unlike the outgoing and praising Jackknife, whom I had ridden with three times by then, Hollywood was a cool character that was always very reserved, not that he holds anything back. He would always say exactly what he thought. I pulled off this flawless ride and he said not a word, good, bad, or otherwise, so, I wasn't about to go fishing for compliments or criticism. I just wanted to get in as many rides as I could, possibly some on my own, securing intersections and highways, before I had to go back to full time work for my brother-in-law or went to find some other dead end job to tide me over, somehow scraping by on minimum wage.

I was told that before our next ride, we would do evals on a closed course. For everybody. Not just the new guys. This would be interesting.

 **EVALS**

Sunday, June 2nd, were the first evals I was a part of. All the riders on the payroll were required to maneuver their way through two elaborate obstacle courses of orange cones. The first half of the day was spent getting to know the first course and practice going through it on the cop bikes. The trickiest part was two hard turns, 90 degrees to the left, then 90 to the right. I tipped the bike over twice in my practice runs, but didn't feel bad about it, just picked it back up and got back on the horse. Sometimes gas would spill out and the bike would have to rest a while before restarting a flooded engine. What was interesting was that other riders who had months or years of experience with the company, were also tipping over the heavy Kawasaki cycles in the tight turns. Everybody could get the first hard left, but it was the following 90 degree hard right that most of us were finding impossible. Once I started seeing other experienced riders dump their bikes, I didn't feel like such an inadequate, inexperienced rider who couldn't tame the beast. It was happening to the best of them and that was because the situation was a tough one, meant to thoroughly test our skills and expose our weak points.

When it came time to be evaluated, each rider would take his turn running the course alone. You started with X number of points, which would be deducted for knocking over cones, by going the wrong way around them, or putting a foot on the ground. It was conceivable to blow the entire course, so we were given two shots to get our best performance in, and the scores would be averaged. On the sidelines, the experienced riders were catching the event on video for Hollywood's scrutiny and feedback. So, we were partially being evaluated in playback, as well as the initial scoring. We were told ahead of time, that if our evals weren't very good, we weren't going to lose our jobs, it was meant to improve our skills. If it had meant our jobs, I probably would have been unemployed again.

Fortunately, I had a chance to ride in the adjacent parking lot and practice my hard leaning tight turning. I would lean over as far as I could to maintain the cornering, which was surprisingly tight. Within a couple minutes I was scraping the running boards (what you rest your feet on) on the pavement through the entire half circle and into the next, basically doing a figure 8, equally well in both the left and right turns. It was a real confidence builder. To hear that scraping sound, metal on asphalt, which is so counter-intuitive at first, it sounds like you're doing something wrong, but you're actually doing it right and doing it well. It felt like you were tearing up the street, literally, and sounded like it too. Getting over that counter-intuitive feeling made you have the opposite feeling, that the rough sound was the sound of doing it right and tearing it up.

I was third to go of the ten or so guys. I pretty much aced the first course, knocked over only a cone or two, put a foot down maybe once. But for the life of me, I couldn't make that second tight right turn and would end up going wide and missing a few cones. At least I didn't tip it over, because that's a total blowing of the course. I felt pretty good about my runs.

Other experienced riders were not so lucky in the hairpin. Handyman was a longtime Washington state motorcycle cop and his riding skill proved it. He took the left turn well, but lost his momentum setting up for the right. The formula's always the same: Lose your inertia in a hard, slow turn and you'll go over. Just as he was about to tip over, he gave it too much throttle to correct and his back wheel burned out from under him and he wiped out in a wild spin that was fun to watch. Gas spilled from the tank onto the pavement. They quickly got the bike up and out of there. Hump came in with a Zippo and lit the gas. Flames burning on the course had us all howling laughing. We weren't getting paid for this day but man, you could sell tickets for this.

We were rolling laughing all day long. Some performances on the course, especially by that of Hollywood and a Clark County Sheriff were amazing, virtually flawless, but not even theirs were perfect. Even the best would knock over a cone or two or put a foot down.

After everybody got their two runs in we took an hour break for lunch. I raced the ten miles back home at mach speed, tear-assing across town as was now part of my increased ability and confidence in my skills. I was in my apartment for only ten minutes, enough time to crush some ice into water and feed the cat. It took me fifteen minutes to get back. I was early, but they had already set up the second course and all five or six bikes were making the rounds through the cones at varied intervals. Sometimes they would screw up because they were just learning the moves and finding their weak spots, but I mostly didn't know when they were screwing up, and when I did know, I didn't know what they intended. The riders on the sidelines explained to me the turns and requirements, but I was really having a difficult time seeing it. Having a problem conceptualizing the route was something that would stay with me to my last ride for the company. There were a lot of cones out there, and if you didn't know exactly what you were supposed to do, it was very confusing and I, was very confused.

THEY WANTED to get started and get back to their lives. Hollywood took the extra time to walk me through the course and show me what was expected. An excellent teacher, Hollywood never spoke down to me or said a word about my timing. Like I said, I got back early, but they were itching to go. In retrospect, it's easy for me to say I shouldn't have gone anywhere during the break but down the street. Standing on the side, watching everyone go through the paces, I still had a difficult time imagining the turns. To me, it's one thing to understand the course from a fixed perspective and watch someone else go through it, and it's something completely different to see it all from the moving point of view of the bike. I felt like I was too stupid to put the two together.

I even videotaped a half dozen run-throughs by Hump until either the tape or the battery ran out and the screen just went blank. I was second to last to go before Hollywood. On my first attempt I got through the initial weaving part which was to me obvious and simple, into a set of tight, slow turns where I was blank on where to go next, slowing to a stop and putting a foot down. I blew my first try so distinctly that I couldn't count the run. My second attempt went much the same, I got lost in the cones and didn't know the next turn. I had boned it so bad there probably wasn't a score to count. My frustration with myself just got worse. I knew I could do this stuff, the physical handling of the bike to get it through the paces, but I didn't know the course well enough to pull it off and was getting very upset that I couldn't show it.

On a rare third try I got through the course further and

without much flaw, but when I reached a series of cones for a clockwise and then counter figure eight, I screwed the pooch and yelled out "SHIT!!" loud enough to be heard by everyone. I was pissed and it was clearly conveyed by my tone of voice. It had that 'I want to kill somebody, especially myself' sound to it. Once again, it's easy for me to say I wish I hadn't done that and that it's one of those things I'm always trying to control but, sometimes I fail. When I fail, it's usually not a pretty picture. I was in fact, very glad to know that my defeat on those second course trials weren't preserved on videotape and will just be remembered as the tries where I fucked up. It bothered me further that my one word outburst caused me to stand out in a not-so positive way. Hollywood told me in a constructive light that I was being too hard on myself and stressing too much about it. I took the advice of the other riders and left my concern behind on the course. At the end of the day we had no real feedback about our trials and most of us would have to eagerly await more detailed instruction on our weak points to work on.

I didn't have to wait long. Monday I had a ride of a relatively short distance. I showed up at the office an hour and a half ahead of time. Jackknife showed up about thirty minutes before takeoff time. One of the first things he said to me was, "I've got three words for you: Let it go." with a smile. Letting it go meant to me that it was yesterday and that it was a day separate from today. I still was itching to prove my abilities and earn the respect of this elite group of motorcycle riders that was unique unto all others.

The garage at Oregon Funeral Service, known as O.F.S., was a relatively small, all in one kind of space that reflected the size of the operation. It was a small outfit and had a lean crew feeling to it. There wasn't any sense of some huge corporate entity, it felt more like a family business that was more about providing a needed service than making money. There was enough room for a limo or two, a few bikes, some big metal coolers where bodies of the deceased were sometimes kept, and a locker area to get changed at, along with a tool rack with things like oil and chain lube. A few steps from the locker space was a little break room, big enough, but kind of cramped if five or so people were there. Beyond that, there was the office and entrance where dispatch worked out of.

A plain unmarked white van backed into the garage and when it parked, two guys hopped out wearing industrial coveralls, like they were technicians of some kind. Between the nondescript van and their equally unidentifiable clothes, there was aura of mystery about them. They were known as the first call people because they're the first ones who get the call when a body needs to be picked up and taken somewhere. Sometimes that somewhere was here at our garage. From the back of the van, they unloaded a body wrapped in white industrial-quality plastic, thicker than a Hefty garbage bag. A Caucasian foot could be seen through the plastic at the end with a pink toe tag on it. Jackknife helped the driver lift the body onto a table that would be wheeled into the cooler. That was something I thought to myself I would never do and was pretty well grossed out at the sight of it. Occasionally help lift dead bodies wasn't something I remember being in the job description.

It was another sweltering day with a muggy, high humidity. Rare for Oregon. It was a service for a Black person in a rough Portland neighborhood. Riding with Jackknife and Aerosmith, I got to play a more active role in securing intersections, savoring jamming at the unflinching oncoming traffic, even though I'm coming at them at nearly fifty miles an hour with all my lights going. Despite having lots of red lights flashing, swirling, hazards blinking, some cars get frustrated at the notion of stopping even momentarily and jam right back at me in defiance. Pure American attitude. Oncoming buses sometimes thought nothing of me and didn't give me any margin for error; I squeaked by one with only inches to spare.

The procession was only a dozen cars or so, visibility was excellent, roads were dry as a bleached desert bone. I was riding tandem next to Jackknife, a few car lengths ahead of the hearse. I heard over the lousy radio earpieces Jackknife call to me "The next intersection's all yours. Go get it!" I felt like a dog that had been let off its leash to fetch a far away bone before some other hound got it. I gunned the bike ahead at insane speed because there was nothing standing between me and the green light. I got into the intersection blowing the whistle full blast to get everyone's attention. Once they've all seen me and have stopped or made their move, I hold up my clenched fist to signal to the biker leading the hearse that it's secure to come through.

The ride went smooth and without flaw. We reached the cemetery and parked our bikes parallel to each other in the oncoming traffic lane to secure it and stood between the bikes and the procession pulling into the cemetery. There was a minor delay when the hearse pulled into the grounds and didn't know which way to go. They looked for the lead car to navigate them to the gravesite but it wasn't ready, didn't know what it was doing. Most of the procession was stuck sitting in the lane wondering what the hell the holdup was, as was I. It was as if the guys didn't know the procession was coming.

Mission complete, we started on our way back to the office with the sense of euphoria that is inherent with an excellent ride. I can only speak for myself, but an element of pride comes after such a successful run. On the roads and the highways, people see us in their rear view mirrors and get out of the way, worried they might get caught speeding or something. They get out of the fast lane so we can go screaming by them at fifteen miles an hour over the posted limit. It's rides like today's that I feel are too short and wish could last longer. I only had four rides under my belt and wished I could spend the rest of the day riding around getting a better feel for the bikes and working on technique, clutch and throttle control, tight slow turning, balance issues and things like that. -But that wasn't an option and I just had to wait until the next ride. Other than the evals in the parking lot, all the learning I was going to get was going to be on the job.

In the garage, I gently moved the bike into an open spot between the limos and other bikes. At the end of these rides, I'm usually wound up and psyched and can't get enough coffee in me. As was a reflection of my life at the time, I didn't have anything pertinent to go to afterwards. As I was meandering around the garage, getting things straightened out, mileage checked, radio checked back in, all that stuff, I took a look at the board listing the 'deliveries' of the past week or so. Under the listing of the method of interment, someone had twice written creamation. C-R-E-A-M-A-T-I-O-N. Think my head tilted a bit as I looked at it, like a confused dog. Back then, as now, whiteboards don't come with spellcheck.

RIDE 6 - 7

It was gorgeous summer weather, a Thursday, and Portland was in a cut loose atmosphere. Rose Festival was behind us and the best of the season lay ahead. The two other riders who would be showing me the ropes would soon be leaving the company, one to become a full time father, the other because he was moving out of town. The day was a double header, one funeral and then another. I got to the garage around 9 in the morning, did all the pre-run checks, lubed the chain, got coffee for my tombstone mug, checked out a walkie-talkie, found a suitable helmet, all the usual stuff.

The two other riders were both non-police civilians like myself. They showed up with time to spare and suddenly I was the one scrambling to get my helmet on and the bike revved to get out the door. They went down to the Texaco down the street without waiting for me, even though we weren't late at all.

After pumping my gas, the guy behind the counter punched in the wrong code and told me that I had an invalid number, which I knew wasn't right, but how could I prove it? I whipped out my own money just to get out of there, but he entered the number again, this time correctly, and it went through no problem, the cashier realizing his mistake. His apology couldn't make up for the precious minutes his delay caused, which fell on me. It seemed as if I were hanging them up, one rider saying, "We don't have time for this shit."

We got out to the chapel in the heart of Portland and waited for the service to end. I handed out the orange funeral papers to the people coming out of the church. It's weird when you ask older people, "Are you going to the cemetery?" They're coming out of a traumatic event, dazed and confused over their loss, and I have to hit them with this question. More often than not, the answer is "Huh?"

The procession to the cemetery was relatively short and without mishap. I was bumping just about every intersection. Hold one light until the last car goes by, then take off back up to the front and secure the next light before the hearse gets there. So, one run in the bag, one to go.

Our next ride was a service going from Gladstone to Newberg; a pretty long haul, the procession was nearly two dozen cars and the route would have no shortage of things to try and trip us up.

Before we got to the location, the guys wanted to stop at a Taco Bell in Tigard, which was another strange scene; we look like cops on and off the bikes. I've never seen three motorcycle cops come into a Taco Bell and snarf down burritos and neither had the people in the restaurant, but we were so hungry, we barely paid attention to all the looks we were getting.

So, lunch break over, we walked back to our bikes and as we discussed the anticipated route, consulting the map, which was a Thomas Guide by the way, you know, like paper maps in a book, a woman pulled into the parking lot and got out of her car, holding her young daughter in her arms. She came up to us saying, "Excuse me, officers? My daughter woke up the other day crying. She said she's been having nightmares where police officers were the bad guys. I have no idea why she thinks this. Could you talk to her?" With a smile and a charming voice one rider tried his best to draw the girl out but couldn't get her to say her own name or anything else. Quite content at the effort, the mother thanked us and went on her way.

Riding through the city of Tualatin I passed a Kerr contractors construction crew that I might have been working with if I weren't riding. When we got to the chapel in Glad-stone, the service hadn't started and people were still showing up. The family members were more distraught than usual. Quiet, but visibly distraught. This is common when the person's death is a tragedy, taken too young or unjustly, unlike someone who lived to be 95 and passed in their sleep.

Then I saw a laserprint of a young guy's face in the window of a car parked in the lot. I recognized the face from the news but couldn't recall the details. It wasn't long before I learned that the guy had been killed when he jumped into a river at the place notoriously known as High Rocks. Death at High Rocks by drunken swimmers and divers is an annual occurrence and this guy was its latest victim.

The family was one that you could tell appreciated motor-cycles and rock and roll. The father of the 25 year old deceased was wearing blue jeans and a Harley t-shirt. Some of the girls there were knockout gorgeous, but funerals are no place for romance or flirtation. There were a lot of tattoos to go around too. You see the little kids being led by the hand and think of the tattoos they will have not so many years from now. Skulls on their shoulders with a snake writhing out an eye socket, their favorite band names and maybe some ex-girl-friends they thought they'd be together with forever.

The service was especially long and we had an hour of time to kill. As guys often do, we mostly talked about women, relating experiences, good and bad. We were having our laughs and sometimes you have to keep yourself in check from laughing too loud at anything. It's just not the place for that, just as attempted romance at a funeral is in really bad form. That's why if you're told an excellent joke that especially amuses you at a funeral service, it takes some effort to keep from cracking up too much. It could be the funniest thing you've ever heard in your life and you have to act like it wasn't.

The service was taking a lot longer than expected and one rider went inside to see what was going on. He came back out smiling, telling us that someone was playing Led Zeppelin full blast on a boom box at the end of the service. He said that every person over fifty had their fingers in their ears.

I stood outside the main door where people were coming out from the service, orange funeral papers in hand. Despite the volume, apparently Zeppelin went over big because there wasn't a dry eye walking out those doors. I got the usual responses from the family and friends as they came out, wiping away their tears. I would ask, "Are you going to the cemetery?"

"W-what?"

"Will you be going to the cemetery?"

"Yeah."

Handing them the paper, I'd say, "Just put this on your dashboard and turn on your lights, please."

They take the paper and usually walk a few dazed steps until they're hugged by a close family member or someone they haven't seen in a long time. The very young children hardly have any idea what's going on and can't figure out why everyone seems to be so sad. I caught part of the character of the deceased guy's family and friends when I heard one person ask the whereabouts of someone expected to make the service. The answer was, "He hasn't been released yet."

The coffin was loaded into the hearse and the funeral director was given a walkie-talkie. He fired up the red swirling dashboard light and I pulled into the right lane at 45 degrees, securing the lane for the procession to drive into, and blew the whistle. An oncoming car saw my upraised hand, police motorcycle with flashing lights, and stopped. Another rider stopped the cars in the oncoming left lane, while the other rider lead the hearse and the procession out of the chapel parking lot into the street to the highway. The last car went by and I jammed out of there at full speed to reach the front. This is where I should point out the importance of getting to the front as soon as humanly possible. In front of the hearse is the safest place to be, being the first to get into the intersection or the on-ramp is prime. The faster you can get to the front the better, because coming up from behind the left side of the procession, against oncoming traffic in a narrow corridor, these things happen quick and you want to get out of that window of danger as soon as possible.

It's easy to say that the procession can always stop and wait for a red light, since the riders haven't been able to reach the front, but some hearse drivers think they're on a mission ordained by some higher power and therefore have the God-given right to blow through red lights, as if everybody driving around Portland that day should just magically 'know' they're coming. This is how accidents happen, people get hurt, or worse.

I got to hold the traffic from the I-205 on ramp as the procession merged into the slow lane as a single flowing unit. When the last car with its headlights on and an orange paper in the window went by, I could see it was a pretty long line of cars. I took off and got into fifth gear in nothing flat, jumping between the two solid lanes of virtually bumper to bumper traffic that was moving at about 45 miles an hour. I tore ass up the center of the two lanes under the assumption nobody would be changing lanes, nobody had any turn signals blinking and there was no room to move. With maybe a foot of space on each side between the cars of two lanes, I glanced down to my speedometer and saw myself doing 85 miles an hour. I passed two dozen cars in moments, then hit the brakes and swerved into place a car length in front of the hearse, taking up half a lane beside another rider. In retrospect, that was one of the ballsiest, most skillful moves I ever pulled.

It was on a stretch of I-205 right outside my parent's house in West Linn, and that one sprint alone stands out in my mind as one of the greatest rushes of my life. Just a moment where it was so great to be alive and doing this.

These families who clearly appreciated motorcycles were watching us all the way. People in the procession sometimes watch you closely because they're usually driving slower than the speed limit in a relatively straight line. It's so easy for them that it's boring and they watch us come screaming by at a million miles an hour, we must appear as a blur. Then they see us sitting in the center of an intersection as they drive by, anticipating us to come screaming by again at any moment. They're just driving along at their ho-hum pace and then 'Schzooooom!', we come ripping by. Some have the courtesy and foresight to stay to the right side of the lane to give us room. I appreciate those people.

We turned into I-5 and took the first exit through Tualatin. I was directed to secure the first intersection and when I got to the base of the hill, I overshot the center of the four-way intersection by about ten feet, which made my traffic control position worthless. Not enough people could see me because it would be virtually impossible to get their attention. The hearse comes rolling by without knowing I hadn't secured the traffic, so my second mistake in a matter of split second timing was not calling over the walkie talkie that the intersection wasn't secure. The two riders behind me came through the street not knowing I had not been able to make eye contact with all the cars. One car unexpectedly pulled out in front of a rider and he knew instantly that I'd screwed up. He pulled up right beside me and yelled, "What happened?!"

"I overshot the middle. I fucked up."

I felt like an idiot from that moment on. I destroyed an otherwise flawless set of rides in an instant and kept myself pegged as a break-in rider for still another day. It's as if I knew graduation from that status would be postponed, like a goal line being stretched out away from you as you run toward it.

The ride through Tualatin and Sherwood to Newberg went without further incident, except that as the lead bike, I was directed to go forward when the hearse took the final left into the cemetery which was out of sight. I was rolling forward slowly when a rider came beside me and said, "Turn around."

"Huh?"

"Turn around!"

I followed him back to the road the hearse was taking into the cemetery. We screamed up in front of the hearse and parked our bikes parallel outside the gate, the procession driving into the photogenic pioneer cemetery one by one.

On the way back to the office, we were riding along the highway through Tigard past Beef Bend Road, the road I grew up on, and coincidentally, the road I would have been working at if I weren't riding. I saw the flagging company flagger in my place holding a slow sign and looking very bored. I knew two things for sure, he was making a hell of a lot more money than I was, but I had the thrill of a lifetime while he was standing there probably wondering where his life was going. I had showed up at the office initially at 9 am. We got back there at 4:30, a hundred miles later. At the end of the day, I would have $14 to show for it. 14 bucks for a full day wasn't going to pay the rent, but I would have gladly paid that much to have had the experiences I had that day.

 **RIDE 8 - 9**

I called the office message and heard about Handyman being injured, called the next day and got some sketchy details, but the chilling feeling of knowing that it happens to the best of them was sobering. The day it happened had been perfect weather, visibility: ideal. I figured if it could happen to him in perfect conditions, how likely was it that it could happen to me under worse circumstances?

It was the day before my 28th birthday and a beautiful Saturday morning. Partly cloudy skies, silver linings everywhere. Riding with Jackknife, we went downtown to a funeral for a Cambodian American man who was murdered by another Cambodian trying to shoot his ex-wife. The victim got in the way, trying to protect the woman he was sheltering from the former husband. The killer shot the man, the woman and her child survived, then he shot himself in a suicide. *His* body was refused by the church and sent somewhere else to get a murderer's burial or cremation.

.   .   .

JACKKNIFE EXPLAINED the course we'd take to get on the highway for the short run to the cemetery and Hump thought he understood. I'm sure he understood better than I did, because even though the streets Jackknife referred to were only a few blocks away, and I'd traveled on them many times, I'd never noticed the signs. I couldn't see it in my head, and lord knows, I couldn't remember the names of the streets and what direction we'd go when we got there. North, South, East, West, what am I, a migrating goose? My memory is terrible. I can't remember telephone numbers between the time I look at the phone book to the time I start dialing. And this is back when we had phone books...

We got the procession going slowly through the stop and go part of downtown, lights at every block between the church and the highway. I jammed up to the front, missing the hold of a green light that quickly turned red. One of our guys already being there, I went to the next green light and held that one. The hearse and procession went rolling by smoothly. Hump came speeding by me and up the hill. The hearse lead the procession onto the highway and we were looking alright, but then everything unraveled.

The highway was crammed with cars. I sped around the procession, through a tunnel, searching the jammed up traffic for the lead car, the hearse. It was nowhere in sight when I got out of the tunnel and all four lanes were filled with cars that had no idea there was a procession going on. Cars were moving around and people were changing lanes without signaling, it was ugly. Jackknife came up around me through an opening and I followed him up to the front.

"Where's Hump?!" He asked.

"I thought you were him!"

Jackknife stood up on the footplates but couldn't see Hump anywhere ahead. He called over the walkie-talkie for him a number of times, "Hump, hey where are you?"

Finally the response came, "I'm on Third." which didn't seem to make any sense at all, because we got on the highway at 13th, and 3rd was a half mile of red lights across downtown. You see, one important thing is that even though Hump is on a cop-looking bike, he can't hit the siren or go through stop lights to catch up. He has to wait for greens just like everybody else. One thing was for sure, he was still downtown and to try to catch up to the front with us, would be asinine. Jackknife and I handled it the rest of the way without any scrapes. The radio communication once again was terrible, and I could hardly understand a thing. Just goes to show that when things are going right, two riders are enough, but when things are working against you, you need three or more.

HUMP DID EVENTUALLY CATCH up with us and we stopped at a Burger King a few miles inside of Washington state. The parking lot was full of people and cars coming and going, every single one of them staring at us like the circus had just hit town. Most people were surprised to see three motorcycle cops pull into a fast food place, but this reception was like hailing the Clint Eastwood character in a spaghetti western where the townsfolk have been bullied too long and are waiting for a gunslinger or the seven samurai to deliver them. What made our reception understandable is that the cities and counties of southern Washington don't have motorcycle cops, so we seemed like something new and completely unfamiliar to them. People stopped their cars to ask us questions as they were pulling out, bringing the parking lot to a standstill. Kids jumped out of their parent's cars to run up to us and ask us about guns and motorcycles.

Inside the place was no different. The three of us hardly had time to eat or drink anything between the barrage of inquiries from kids and adults alike. What a difference a badge makes. If I was sitting there in the same leather and clothes, no one would notice me whatsoever and I would be completely ignored. But a police badge and a beat up cop helmet with a walkie-talkie is all it takes to ensure the people will be looking at you as if you're the Man With No Name that has come to save the place.

WHILE WAITING for the service to finish at the funeral home, a little kid, maybe 9 years old, limped down the slanted ramp at the back door and wanted to talk, telling me how he had accidentally shot his foot with a high-powered bb gun. He was playing with his mother's huge jangle of keys, at least a dozen of them on a big silver hoop, tossing them around on his wrist to entertain himself with the noise they made. He was asking more questions than I had time to answer until he suddenly dropped the noisy mess of metal on to his bad foot and cried out "Oooow!" It was all I could do not to laugh at this accident prone kid. That was my cue to cut the conversation short and get on with the procession.

Once on the road, leading the procession in tandem with Hump, in one tight turn we were taking overly fast, he nearly ran me off the road coming in so close. We were supposed to be riding parallel to each other but he would either ride too far ahead or behind me to get any kind of consistency to what he was doing. Even though he had a lot more experience than I did riding such big bikes, but only a few more rides than I did on the job, he was clearly on a power trip.

Jackknife noticed that he really liked the psuedo-cop look the job and uniform gave us. Before the procession got under way, Hump had positioned himself up the street, trying to exude authority unnecessarily over the passing traffic, trying to make them slow down with his stern disapproving body language on the side of the road.

It wasn't long before we were cruising through this spectacular view of the Columbia River Gorge, a single lane corridor hugging the banks of the vast body of water, a sheer vertical rock face on the left and the sterling blue river to the right. Little fishing shacks with short wooden docks dotted the shore line. How peaceful those little oases of heaven must have been to whomever got to fish there, legs dangling over the edge with a line in the water. It was one of the most serene moments of all the rides I had, so fleeting and unexpected, it's suddenly upon you and then it's gone.

Jackknife told me to go on up ahead to find the road to the cemetery. I put it in fourth gear and took off. Far up the street on my own, I saw the Bunker Hill Road sign and shortly thereafter a narrow, steep unpaved road leading up the hill and out of sight. I looked in my mirrors and waited until I saw the bikes leading the hearse way behind me. I called over the radio to the funeral director, the only one who had been to the cemetery and knew where it was, "Hey, is this little sidestreet it?"

The funeral director responded, "Yep. That's it."

I went halfway up the hill when Jackknife called out, "No! That's not it. Turn around." It wasn't a scolding comment, just... accurate. Bunker Hill was another hundred feet down the main road. Me, where I was, up on this steep hill, was a tough place to stop and try to turn around. I got her in neutral and gently tried to muscle the bike back around, but any mistake would be costly on such an incline. While backing up, my rear wheel went slightly downward off the edge of the road and when I gave it some gas, the wheel went to work digging itself into the soft ground. I was screwed, stuck as could be and needed some help to get out of there. Anything I was going to try to do by myself was just going to make things worse.

The procession of cars passed by down on the main street

below, probably wondering what the hell I was doing up on this hill. -Enjoying the view? Or did I really think someone was going to come down this rural hilltop road and interrupt the procession? I had to deliver the news, "You're not going to believe this but, I'm stuck." I heard Jackknife laugh in sympathy, knowing the funeral director had misguided me up the Bad Hill, which was clearly not Bunker Hill.

Jackknife said, "Just hang on there, Steve. We'll come and get you on the way back."

"Copy that." I said. And I sat there and waited, feeling like an idiot. Not even thirty seconds go by and a big red pickup comes down the road at me and I wave it around. Instead, the father and son stop and get out of the car and walk down to me, the father saying, "Saw you down here and saw you get stuck."

"Hey thanks!" I said, hardly believing my luck. They lifted the back end of the bike and I gently gave it enough gas to creep out of the ditch and back down the road.

"Thanks a million!" I said, as I took off to catch up with the procession that was now far out of sight.

I came over the radio, "O.K. you guys, I'm free and comin' at ya."

The response was, "Good. Careful coming up around these corners, there's gravel and the cars are bunching up. We're coming into the cemetery now."

"Right. Thanks." I jam up the curvy hills to the left of the procession and reach the top where the cars are slowly turning one by one into the cemetery. We wait until the last car goes by and then regroup, shut off the cycles for a minute. Atop Bunker Hill the view of the surrounding countryside was magnificent, nothing but green trees as far the eye could see in all directions. I was taken by the beauty of the scene, so tranquil and in touch with nature. Again, those fleeting unexpected moments.... The pallbearers walked the coffin to the

rectangular hole in the ground, somber as could be. Jackknife
had a laugh about how I got out of the spot I was in and said,
"Alright, let's get out of here." And rightly so.

AT THE TEXACO IN KALAMA, Washington, Hump said to me in
an intimidating way, "Just keep up with me." as if to say, 'Keep
up with me and my every move, or else.' I didn't say anything
because I knew he was way out of line. It was then obvious
that he had no respect for me and thought I would need
frequent scoldings and would be worthy of second guessing of
my understanding and abilities. That was the first time I felt
aggravation or stress on the job as a result of another rider. I
don't know who he thought he was, but the job, the bike, the
uniform and the badge was clearly going to his head.

I was point man on the 50 miles back to Portland from
Kalama, with Jackknife and Hump following in tandem behind
me. I stayed around 70 to 80 miles an hour for most of the
way, until I saw Jackknife in the my mirror flashing all five
fingers of his hand twice. At first I thought he was trying to get
my attention without the radio or that something was flashing
on my bike, but it took a second to realize that the speed limit
had decreased from 70 to 60 a mile or so ago. I took it down to
60 and watched the traffic ahead of me, seeing my bike in their
rear view mirrors and moving over to the center lane. Nobody
wants a speeding ticket.

BACK AT THE garage I saw Handyman, his right eye all cut up
and ugly with stitches. He didn't seem to think too much if it
though... I heard the story about how the guy leading the
procession left the downed rider, Handyman, behind and
continued on, when a motorist, an off-duty nurse, stopped and
stayed with him until an ambulance showed up. He was taken

to the hospital, cat-scanned, things like that, and received 27 stitches around his eye from a plastic surgeon. Such were the potential hazards involved with the job, but after a day like the one I had that day, you couldn't wait for what might happen tomorrow.

 **RIDE 10 - 11**

I called the motorcycle dispatch number from my parent's house on my birthday and found I had two rides the next day with Hump and Hollywood. Right off the bat I knew it would be a scrutinizing two trips. I figured if I fucked up really bad, Hump would be all-too willing to point out my weaknesses to Hollywood and I'd be toast. On the message it said, blah blah blah blah "Hollywood, Hump and Steve Edwards as a break in... " SIGH. Keyword: Break in. Seriously? I think the last two rides I wasn't listed as a break in, but couldn't be sure. I was doing more than typical break in rides, would be the first to arrive in an intersection and hold it, as opposed to bumping, where you fill in for someone who has already got the intersection secured. -That's breaking in. This felt like I had been knocked down a peg or two, as if demoted or something. Everybody stops being a break in and becomes a normal rider at a different point, some earlier than others, and mine was taking an extra long time as far as I was concerned. But, they knew better than me and were thinking of my and their safety first, more so than my sense of pride.

I geared up the bike I was assigned and did all the pre-run checks. I was there before any other rider going out that day, which wasn't unusual. After topping off the oil, lubing the chain, and all the other stuff, there was no sign of Hollywood. There was some confusion as to where he would meet us, at the garage or at the service. No one seemed to know. Hump suddenly shows up and says he doesn't want to ride the bike assigned to him, 5-6, and would rather have mine. I'm more than eager to trade bikes because 5-4 is a noisy beast whose red light swirling on the front makes a bothersome grinding noise, like "Gwwooow-wwoooww-wwoooww" that makes me feel like I consistently get assigned the bike no one wants and is the one that would be the most expendable. I did the pre-run checks on Hump's bike in a hurry and we sped out of there as if we were late.

We weren't sure of how to get on the highway the best way, so there was some confusion. I was at a loss, couldn't hear over the radio and communication was often too little too late. The walkie talkies, although they were a famous brand and an industry standard, were old and worn out and in serious need of replacement. We managed to make it over the slew of on-ramps and merges well enough. Beaverton, the home of Nike, was a nightmare from the directions I had; they were from an off duty rider who described every change of highway and road in a generic, simple way, no east or west, right or left, just telling me the changes as if all the turns would be *obvious*. They were not, and Hump was getting his reassurance that somehow *I* was the idiot. We had to pull over and turn around a few times because we were like rats lost in a maze looking for the cheese. Jackknife was the hearse driver this time and later said the directions I got "Was like the blind leading the blind."

The first ride was the one I had the most fun on. Sure enough, Hollywood was waiting for us there and pretty soon, the service was done and the procession under way. Even though I was bumping, holding the intersection after it's been secured, it still meant that I would be there until the last car passed and then jam to the front again, and that's the best part. Screaming up the oncoming traffic lane with almost every car and truck coming at you pulling over and stopping. Those that don't stop at least try to give you some room, but sometimes the squeeze is so tight that there isn't six inches spare room on both sides as you're barreling at each as two moving objects at 60 miles an hour. Just to nick an oncoming car, truck or bus would mean hitting it at a combined velocity of around 100 miles an hour, which is what you want to avoid at all cost.

We delivered the hearse to the cemetery and Hollywood took us up the street to a quaint restaurant with a nice wooden deck out back. We sat there killing time under the umbrella shade drinking ice water and tea. The people sitting around us got in their initial looks of surprise but then largely ignored us, which was nice. -Be able to sit around and shoot the shit, forget about our uniforms and how we looked. At one point where the conversation was running dry I said to Hollywood, "So, when you hired us (me and Hump), you looked over about two dozen applications. I guess I'm curious, if you hired me, what could the rejects have been like?" That got a laugh out of them. He said that some of them who had 20 years experience came off with cocky attitudes, one saying right off the bat, "I can outride any of you guys right now." Hollywood knew the interview was over with that guy right there but entertained the man's esteem for a little longer. Turns out the man was irate when he found out he didn't get hired. Well, tough shit dude. Hollywood explained that they don't want to spend time and energy to make cocky experienced riders unlearn their bad riding habits. So, by comparison, I was a clean slate.

We rode through my hometown of Tigard, over the steep,

winding backroads of the countryside suburbs, up and down Bull Mountain Road from one end to the other. This is a road so etched in my memory from childhood experiences that I couldn't go ten feet without thinking of some incident or memory that had a lasting effect on my life. I passed by the house I initially moved into after being adopted around the age of four and it looked very different, quite small and with a terrible, drab brown paint job. I didn't say a word to the other riders about how many connections and roots I had in the ground we were covering. It wasn't my place to reminiscence at somebody else's expense. Just stay focused on where we were going and what needed being done.

The second service was for a white woman who had passed away at the age of 97. She was a founder of the area, profiled for local newspapers late in life, obviously well liked, but nobody was distraught in their grieving. Everything was as it should be, nobody freaking out, children weren't crying, in fact, there weren't many children present despite the deceased woman's numerous children and grandchildren. It was the good death. I mean, here was a woman who lead the fullest of lives for a very long time, anybody who would be overly mourning her passing would be selfish for not letting go.

During the run, my one slight screw up was on the final intersection hold and turn. I saw Hollywood hold the oncoming two lanes of traffic by standing his bike up and getting off the cycle to get everyone's attention. I heard nothing from him on the radio and wasn't sure if he wanted me to pull up behind him or go ahead with Hump. I went ahead with Hump and heard Hollywood say over the radio, "No. No. I wanted you to hold that."

I realized what he wanted only after hearing it and circled back to try and hold what was left of the procession, but it was too late, the last car passed by and Hollywood with it. That was the last hold on the run and I would have been otherwise flaw-less on that course if I had pulled up behind Hollywood and stayed, but I thought he might have said, "No. No. I wanted you to go ahead, I got this." So, SIGH.

We delivered the hearse and the procession to a cemetery in Tualatin that I had driven by a million times in high school, yet had never set foot in it. When the ride was over, Hollywood said, "Guys, it's been a pleasure." and took off because he lived not far away. Hump and I rode through Tualatin and he asked if I minded if he stopped in at his girlfriend's workplace to pick up some important papers. Coincidently, the construction company I also worked for at the time was across the street from where Hump needed to go. I had to check into the office to see if I was going to work for them the next day. I pulled up and parked the cop motorcycle near the secretary's car outside the office. Of course, I still had on my uniform, badge on my leather, the cop helmet and radio. When I walked in the office, the expression on the two secretaries' faces was priceless. What I would have given to have a picture of their surprise.

I asked if my brother-in-law, Brick, was around, and he was not. Standing right in front of them, the secretaries didn't even recognize me and said, "And you are?" I gave them my name and they came back with, "Steve Edwards? What are you doing like that? I saw this cop park next to my car and wondered what you were coming up here for." I got hold of Brick on the phone and confirmed that I would be needed the next day and left the office. As I was going down the steep stairs, Hump called over the headset, "5-6, this is 5-4, where are you?"

A secretary I didn't recognize was coming up the stairs and she absolutely froze in her tracks and her jaw dropped. I answered Hump as I passed the secretary with her mouth still hanging open, "5-4, took a little longer than I thought. I will be at your location in two minutes or less." I've heard other riders tell of incidents where people have panicked at the sight of the badge and uniform. People literally will sweat and tremble until the officer goes away, especially people that are stoned, drunk or high behind the wheel. I can just imagine what the secretary said when she got back to the office, "*Who was that, and what did he want?!!*"

RIDE 12

On a hot, lazy Sunday afternoon I got a call at home by some guy asking, "Is this Steve Edwards?"

"Yes." I said, which I usually follow up with, "Who's this?" in a demanding tone, but this time I didn't.

"Is this the Steve Edwards who does motorcycle escorts?"

And that got me really apprehensive, who would know about that part of my life and call me up about it?

"Yeah." I said with some reluctance.

"Hey, Steve. This is Hollywood. I'm at home and didn't have your number. I tell you I've called just about every Steve Edwards in the Portland phone book. There's five of 'em."

"This is probably the only time someone has found my name in the phone book for the right reasons." I reply.

So let me take a time out here and explain to you how things were back in the 90s, in case you weren't there, except in the voice of astrophysicist Carl Sagan…

"Imagine if you will, a time when there was such a thing as phone books. Impossibly huge manifests of names and numbers on bible-thin sheets of paper, listing every public name in the city. These troves of personal information, names, addresses and phone numbers, were called 'The White Pages', not to be outdone by The Yellow Pages, an obese collection of business titles and advertising without customer reviews or feedback, just a litany of enterprises, all claiming to be 'Number One' at something, and how we humans crave to be associated with that solitary number, one. Both books, white and yellow, requiring enough pulp and paper to have entire forests fall under the blade, all of which now reside in museums, along with other obsolete artifacts like pagers and fax machines."

HOLLYWOOD TELLS me how the company is short a rider for the next day, really in a tough spot and asking if I could fill in for somebody. Brick was expecting that I would be working for him Monday, but I actually felt the need to put in the necessary ride time to get up to speed.

I wrangled my way out of the construction work and reported the next morning to the garage an hour early as usual. I did all the pre-run checks on my assigned bike and found out that instead of replacing an experienced rider, I would be replacing Hump, who had broken a finger the night before playing with his dogs. The only problem was that it meant I was assigned the monster bike Hump liked so much, which I was willing to trade in a heartbeat.

The three of us left the garage for the gas station down the street in some confusion, the rider CT (as he was called) leaving without really telling us so. We found him filling his tank down the street. I was low on fuel, but the guy I was filling in for and was not there that day had apparently misplaced the gas card or it was in his wallet, so I was up the creek. Had to pay with what little money I had on me. Getting to the service was a piece of cake, but then it was hurry up and wait. Hollywood was getting impatient and wished the service wouldn't take so long only because he and the rest of us wanted to get the show on the road, get to the fun and difficult part.

The pallbearers carried the coffin down the stairs to the hearse and the people began coming out of the church, milling around outside. Sometimes it's difficult to get people's attention for the important distribution of funeral stickers to be placed in the windshield. Often the family and friends haven't seen each other in so long that they're busy saying their hellos, catching up a bit, social stuff at an event that they can't really celebrate. When I'm handing out the papers, most of the time they just hear you say, "If you could just stick this in your windshield," and they usually don't hear the part where you say, "And turn on your headlights."

By the time the hearse gave the go signal, half the procession didn't have their lights or hazards on. I rode back to the end of the line, telling the cars who didn't have their lights on to get around to doing that. Most of them didn't have a clue until I made it very apparent that they hadn't fulfilled their part of the bargain. The procession got under way and my tension level shot right up with it.

I managed to bump the first five intersections, Hollywood and CT taking off waaaay up ahead. It was a surprisingly long procession of cars. For me there was a slight sinking feeling when I pulled up behind another bike and stopped, Hollywood takes off and I look around, re-securing the intersection so that only the procession is moving. There are bogies in the line, cars that have nothing to do with the procession, their turn signals blinking, so I wave them out and they go on their way. I watch the procession in my shaking mirrors as I ride along, the cars with their lights on, and they just keep coming and coming. I see the first car without their lights on and try to jump in between the first car following it, separating the outlier from our group.

Martin Luther King Jr. Road is a long stretch with four

lanes at this point, and cars are pulling out from side streets all over the place, some getting into the procession, more bogies by the minute. Bumping bogies out of the procession is a distraction from getting to the front and securing an intersection, but definitely worth doing if you've got the time. I was cussing under my breath as these unwanted drivers were breaking up the procession, the problem was that it was going over the radio without me knowing. "Fuckin' son of a bitch, shit...Grrrr..." The old, weathered walkie-talkies are sometimes voice activated at random and it can only be brought to your attention by someone else, hearing something that shouldn't be going over the radio. With my walkie talkie unknowingly voice activated, my whistle blowing went over the radio and probably nearly shattered the eardrums of the two other guys, even going over the radio in the hearse. Hollywood got through the static and garble with, "Steve, if you can hear me, switch off your radio." -which in retrospect of how I had nearly blown their ears out, showed incredible restraint on their part for not barking at me or chewing me out just out of sheer frustration or surprise, but in hindsight, they knew it hadn't been my fault.

About a third of the way through the route, MLK turns into McLoughlin Boulevard, where there's only a few traffic lights and you can get some speed going. I'm shifting up into third gear and the rpm's scream out as if I'm doing forty five miles an hour in first. Shifting up to fourth doesn't change anything and it winds out loudly as if I'm torturing it, then suddenly, completely dies. No gas, throttle, electrical, anything, instantly. I come to a sudden stop near CT and try to find neutral, the green light, but I'm not getting anything. No neutral, no start. The bike is dead, dead and dead. I lean the bike over on the kickstand and see the traffic behind me changing lanes to avoid running me over, but my luck wasn't going to hold out forever.

I couldn't find neutral for the life of me and CT told me to get the bike over to the side of the road. I pushed it to the side, the cars left in the back half of the procession I'm sure were wondering what the hell was going on or what was wrong. I kept trying to find neutral, getting nothing at all. CT asked what was up and I said, "It just died on me in third gear. Can't get it in neutral."

The last car passed by and CT had to go. He says, "Stay here. We'll get you on the way back." So I'm left there on the side of the road as CT takes off to race up to the front because Hollywood has got to be at least a mile ahead and wondering what's going on. I can hardly believe it and the neurotic voice in my head gets to work bashing me personally for something that was completely unpreventable and beyond my control. I stood there in the hot sun by the side of the road feeling like a frustrated idiot for the first five minutes, then for the next fifteen I had more time than I wanted to ponder what I could or should be doing with that day. I could be in Tualatin, flagging, making a hundred dollars in one day (which to me was a lot back then), but here I was on the side of the road, making fifteen bucks at best, on a broken down bike, looking like some kind of stranded pseudo-cop. Cars would pass by and I could tell they were wondering what was up, me pacing back and forth off the bike, off the road, not a speedtrap, so what's with that guy?

After what seemed like an eternity, Hollywood and CT returned and took a look at my bike, going straight for the battery and fusebox because there was no electrical signal at all. CT looked under the seat and pulled out one blown fuse, a tiny piece of glass smaller than an inch long. That bitty glass tube with a piece of metal inside had suddenly had too much and blew out, cutting off everything instantly. I asked them if I could have prevented the fuse blowout in a pre-run check and they said no way. The fact that it had started up in the garage was evidence that it was working perfectly. The bike had a history of blowing fuses because of some electrical problem, but it was news to me. Just goes to show how everything can go to shit in an instant, no fault of your own. There are motorcycle parts and then there are motorcycle parts and this one dollar piece of the puzzle was critical to making the bike run like it should. After that day, I would never again underestimate the value of a one dollar part.

 *RIDE 13*

I was supposed to show up some time after 11am, but gung-ho me, I was there just after 9. I got the bike ready and went over the route with Handyman. It was just going to be me and him on one run with only a few cars. Perfect weather and the route would be relatively simple, at least simple enough for Handyman to hold each intersection initially and then I would bump and take over.

At the garage, I knew I was going to open a locker containing a tombstone mug that was a science project of old cold coffee that had reached a point of floating green fungus. And sure enough, there it was. At least it didn't stink unless you put your nose right up to it and really took a whiff, which I didn't do. Lots of riders were gathered in the break room, but I didn't sit down and stood on the outskirts, not feeling it would be in my right place to pour a cup of coffee, pull up a chair and distract them from their conversation. I left the break room with Jackknife and saw an open casket in the corner of the garage and one dead old man at permanent rest inside it.

"Agh!" I cried out. Random flashes of dead people at

unexpected times had not been listed in the job description. A few minutes later the family of the deceased showed up to view his tranquil body before it was sent for cremation.

Handyman told me that I had more time to kill than I expected, so I took my assigned bike down the street with my camera and tripod and set up to get a simple picture at a quiet intersection. Over the course of fifteen minutes, people walked by without saying a word because I wasn't in a public relations mood. Cars slowed to crawl, passing by, gawking. When was the last time you saw what appeared to be a motorcycle cop on the side of the road taking a selfie with a camera on a tripod and 15 foot long air-pressured cable release? I took three shots and was sweating bullets before noon. I got back to the office and polished my boots, got my shirt and whistle on, took a final coffee whiz and started the bike.

On the way out, moments before leaving the garage, a guy asked me and Handyman if one of us could help him get a body out of the freezer and onto a roller. I didn't volunteer and was glad when Handyman stepped forward. The guy rolled out a plastic-wrapped body of a deceased obese man and Handyman said, "It's not that super heavy guy is it?"

"No. This other guy." was the response.

He then wheels out some man dressed in a dark suit, laid in an oblong wood crate. They lifted the crate on the count of three, then Handyman went to warm up his bike. Seeing them lift the open-faced crate wasn't so bad, but I knew then that if I was ever asked if I could help somebody lift a dead body, the answer would be an emphatic NO. Not then, not ever. They couldn't pay me enough to lift dead bodies wrapped in plastic with the toe tags and discolored flesh sticking out the bottom. If that was mandatory, I would have been outta there.

We stopped at the Texaco down the street to fill up as usual. After getting both bikes primed, Handyman's ride wouldn't start. It looked like a battery problem that couldn't readily be solved. I pushed the bike a ways across the station lot and got it going with a compression start. He went back to the office to get the specific bike that I dearly wanted to ride and then filled it up at the station. Obviously the bike he was originally on was operational to an extent, but you can't be at a service, with the procession ready to go, and somebody push starts the lead bike and hopes it doesn't crap out during the ride.

Outside the service, the first people I saw was a woman and her hyper little daughter, who was not fazed in the least by her grandmother's death. She waved a flower in my face, jumping at me, saying "My grandmother died!" with a big, spastic smile on her face like it was a reason for celebration or special attention. She struck me as a poster child for Ritalin, a drug that might just take off some of those obnoxious edges.

Fortunately, the procession was a small one, only a dozen cars at most. I have yet to see a funeral where there wasn't at least one beautiful young or middle-aged woman who I didn't connect eyes with and consider just for a fraction of a second what it would be like; to date, more, whatever. But funerals are never a springing ground for romance, at least not from the perspective of my work, which I agree with. To try to initiate romance in the event of a funeral is callous and disrespectful, not to mention insensitive and a bit repugnant. But looking and wishing is O.K. We can all imagine we were someplace else and if things were different.

I was bumping intersections quickly, one to the next, holding them not much more than 45 seconds at a shot. Racing up to the next intersection against the oncoming traffic was a bit hairy when they wouldn't see me until closing to twenty feet and then they swerve off the road at the last minute, as if I'd somehow snuck up on them with red lights flashing and swirling.

I knew there was a change of plans when Handyman lead us to the Broadway bridge, over a football field's length of steel grating. The slightly under-inflated back tire made the 30 mile an hour crossing a white-knuckler all the way. The bike was weaving all over the place and to go down on steel grating I would imagine is worse than pavement, and worse yet, on a bridge, no escape routes. Chances are, the car behind you or the oncoming won't be able to react in time and would make a pancake out of you. It was hard not to imagine being mushed through the grating like your body was cheese and would fall to the Willamette River below like a pizza topping.

Going up Burnside to Mt. Calvary Cemetery, Handyman stopped leading the procession to yell at a man laying on the sidewalk as if he were dead. Burnside is notorious as the worst street in the city for all variety of lowlifes, but for some reason, this guy that Handyman saw was giving Burnside a bad name. The passed out man was startled awake, saw an actual cop, grabbed his shoes and started walking away, surely only to search for another place to sleep off his hangover or the crash of his high.

Back at the garage I had a chance to talk to Handyman about the ride. In my opinion, it was the first absolutely flawless ride I ever had and made me want to jump in the air and go "Woohoo!" Handyman agreed I did nothing that would constitute messing up. He went on to say that even he screwed up ever so slightly on two occasions, saying the procession would go over the Burnside Bridge when in fact we went over the Broadway. That, and he said we would be taking the 58th street exit on the way back to the office when we actually took 68th. -Two no biggies that are absolutely minor to the point of inconsequence. They were minuscule mistakes he made only because he had to call all the shots, and there were a lot of them. I would probably have made a million more if the run had been entirely on my shoulders.

His face was healing very well I thought. If I didn't know he had been in an accident resulting in 27 stitches, I would have never known anything had happened.

RIDE 14

The 100 degree sweltering weather of two days prior in 24 hours had been knocked down thirty degrees, bringing with it droves of rain. Portland doesn't ever let its residents escape the rain for long. It's almost like being in Hawaii, 80 degrees and sunny, then scattered showers or a downpour in the same day. Only in towns where it rains a lot do the local weather casters come up with incredibly specific terms for rainfall. There's thunderstorms, heavy rain, rain, rain at times, showers, scattered showers, occasional showers, drizzle, mild drizzle, sprinkles, and partial clearing at the upper level low. Today's weather would be classified as scattered showers, heavy at times with partial clearing. In other words, we were going to get soaked at some point along the way, during, or on the way back to the office. It was an inescapable part of motorcycle riding in Oregon.

The service was in Beaverton at some nursing home or something. We arrived in the parking lot and saw no hearse, which typically would have been there well before us. Hollywood told me to wait in the lot as he rode off to look around. I killed the bike and stood it out of the way. A young nurse in the parking lot saw my arrival and kept staring at me with a seductive and intriguing smile I wished I could take home. She kept smiling, drawing closer and said, "Are you guys Washington County?" She obviously had a thing for cops.

"I'm not." I said, "But I believe the other rider is a Portland reservist." Elusive enough I thought, without blowing the whole illusion.

"Oh." she said and tended to her duties. I got the feeling she would have liked to talk some more, but the conditions weren't quite right. You tend to be greeted by the funeral director shortly after arriving and without Hollywood being the point man, I had to be at the ready.

Sure enough, the funeral director promptly showed up and said there was no hearse. Instead, the car that would transport the coffin was an old green 4x4 truck with a canopy; the truck the deceased man had owned and drove. He had modified it with a loud police siren he liked to drive to his friends' homes and sound off when he arrived. A male relative of his once told him, "You keep doing that, somebody's gonna kill you."

I heard Hollywood over the radio calling to dispatch to see if a hearse was en route or what. I felt like I was interjecting but it was necessary, "Hollywood, if you're looking for the hearse, it's a private car back here in the lot."

He came right back and was informed about the green truck. This changed everything. By law, a legal funeral procession consists of a hearse with a red flashing light in the windshield, all the cars in the procession have their lights and hazards on. So Hollywood had to rethink the whole procession right there on the spot, realizing we couldn't do things the way they were normally done. We would be stopping for every red light and waiting, keeping our pursuit lights off until holding the intersection, then flip them on. He'd be in the lead, secure the traffic and then I would roll up behind him and stop, hit the lights and he could take off to get the next one.

The driver of the green truck, who would not be the funeral director that knew the route, would be the male relative I spoke to. As expected, a sudden cloudburst sent buckets of rain our way as we waited for the service to end and the families to get ready.

The driver of the 4x4 came to us and said, "Can I ask a favor of you two? Could you guys stick around when we get to the cemetery? We want to hit the siren when we put him in the ground. We thought he would like that."

When it was made clear we would actually be within the cemetery when he wanted to do this, it was no problem. I couldn't help but think of Dennis Hopper in Apocalypse Now, when the p.t. boat arrives up river at the Kurtz compound and the natives watch in awe, Hopper screaming, "Zap 'em with the siren! Zap 'em with the siren!"

I said to him, "We'll get you all inside the cemetery and then you can zap 'em with the siren to your hearts' content."

I handed out about 15 funeral stickers and we were ready to roll. The only thing to wait for was the deceased man's disabled wife to finish going to the bathroom. A pallbearer asked us if we were hungry, because they had a lot of food to go around, but we declined because to do so undermines your image when carrying out the task at hand. It's just a bad look. You're supposed to be respectable during the service and the ride, but ten minutes ago you were shoveling potato salad down your gullet like a free meal meant more to you than dignity. The ride was uneventful and problem free, which was good, and in the end, he went in the ground to the wail of his beloved siren.

On the way back to the garage, a flagger stopped us in the street at a construction site on Cornell Road that only a few weeks prior I had been flagging to put up detour signs for this very project. Sitting on our bikes waiting, I could see the flagger holding the stop sign only a car's length away was one I had worked with on Beef Bend Road, the street I grew up on. She couldn't recognize me to save her life and I didn't get a chance to say anything to clue her in. Also saw a Multnomah County inspector whom I had worked with on several projects, but she would never be able to recognize me either. It was kind of like Clark Kent Syndrome. You put on some glasses and suddenly, everybody thinks you're a different person.

 **RIDE 15**

Perfect weather and riding with Hollywood. Finally, I was no longer a break in. In fact, a new guy was there on his second ride with Handyman. It was hard to believe there was still anyone greener than me, but apparently there was. I had a funny feeling it wasn't going to take a dozen rides for him to get up to speed like it had for me.

On the way to the service we got on to Interstate 5 and came to a screeching halt with a standstill of bumper to bumper traffic as far as the eye could see. If we had to wait it out, this could mean a huge delay. Hollywood turned on his hazards and lead the way along the shoulder of the road, past hundreds of cars that I'm sure were hoping we had arrived to clear up the situation ahead. We kept passing more and more cars, until we saw two motorcycles off the side of the road with flares burning around them. There was a Portland police car on the side as well, and in the center of four lanes of traffic was a huge r.v. at a dead stop. You really couldn't tell what had happened, but it was a mess, that was for sure. A lot of pissed off people were trying to get around the scene and on their way. Riding past all those cars like we did is something every motorcyclist wants to do in those situations, but to get caught would be a hefty fine. And yet, I would imagine to some motorist's dismay, we just rode through it all and took off.

The service was for a Mormon at a Church of Latter-Day Saints. Hollywood and I talked to the funeral director for quite a while, a young guy named Golf, waiting for the service to end. At one point we were laughing so hysterically it's a wonder they didn't hear us inside and tell us to shut up.

The procession was going smoothly enough until the last leg, where I had to get ahead of the hearse and help them merge onto a fast highway. What you do is get ahead of the procession, get on the highway and hold the merging lane by going slowly so cars will go around you and the procession can just cruise easily into the right side lane. That done, time to get back to the front. When I was almost there, right beside the hearse, kind of between lanes, I looked in my mirror and saw a car screaming up behind me at 60 miles an hour. It came ripping by and missed me by *inches*; you know, like the length of a finger. I nearly bounced off the hearse, not taking time to see the expression on the driver's face, but I'm sure it was momentary terror.

I mean, it was super dangerous and I had to get out of there before I got creamed. Getting dinged doing 60 on a highway full of cars doing 55 would be a disaster, really high speed and more than likely not just one car involved, but lots. There may be no oncoming traffic on a major highway, but it has plenty of its own dangers with everybody rushing to go in the same direction. That near miss closely averted, I got in the lead and took the exit we needed, the hearse and everyone in tow back in the relative tranquility of city streets. Not far away was the cemetery where the staff was patiently waiting for the new resident to check in for the first and final time. For Hollywood, I'm sure it was just another day, just another ride, but for me it was an invaluable learning experience to go from being less green to a more seasoned rider who'd seen and done it all.

FUNERAL RIDE 16

A *beautiful* day. The last ride was a week and a half ago. Employment was virtually non-existent in those nine or so days, I had worked four hours over two days for my construction company. That's the nature of flagging, it can be a couple hours one day, a couple hours another. But paying the rent? Ha.

I called the company message line for the next day's rides from my parent's house and heard it say that the three Steves would be riding together for the first time, followed up with something like 'The Three Amigos'. There was a long pause, giving time to hear the reluctant echoes of laughter in the office. Like a bad dad joke falling flat, laughing at the attempt more than anything else.

It was a smooth procession from southeast Portland to Willamette National Cemetery, the big military cemetery up on the hill. After arriving, Handyman, Hollywood and I, along with the funeral director, couldn't help but get into conversation that lead to howling laughs. You gotta love 'em for having a great sense of humor. We were standing out there in the hot afternoon sun for an hour or so before the service got out and an elderly crowd slowly shuffled out. No looks of surprise or tragedy here. I welcome such a mood because it allows you to be more relaxed and listened to by the attendees. People can actually pay attention when they aren't so grief-stricken and devastated by the loss of a loved one.

As people were starting to leave the church from the rear exit, Hollywood told me to take the bike around back and hand out the orange funeral papers to the people who had no idea how we were all going to get to the cemetery. I tucked the papers into the front of the seat and rode down a steep hill to the lot. In the process, the 70 or so papers were in my lap and it was just luck that they didn't all go spilling into the street like a ticker tape parade. I nearly dumped the bike just going down the hill with one hand holding in the clutch and braking the rear with my foot. Luckily, I managed to take the papers and bite them in my mouth and get to the back without choking on them.

I handed out the papers and saw Hollywood ride around and give me the signal to rock and roll. I got the bike going all good and fine, got into the street with my pursuit and hazard lights all right, but my whistle was still stuffed inside my shirt under my leather. That thing is absolutely necessary if you're going to get people's attention without a siren. Once again, fumbling for something at slow speed nearly caused me to dump the bike, but nobody saw it.

In the procession I made two slight mistakes only because I wondered what specifically was wanted of me and what I thought would be safest. They were minor mistakes but something that had been brought up in the last run, dropping behind the rider in front of the hearse, instead of going up ahead of him to bump the guy holding the intersection. It just seemed like screaming up the lane like a bolt of lightning to slam on the brakes was not what I thought he wanted me to do. Wrong.

Other than the functions performed during the escort part of the runs, half the fun is riding to and from the services in tandem in the same lane. It's just as much a test of your abilities as doing a procession and holding traffic or riding to the front against oncoming cars that sometimes don't know I'm coming until the last second.

I sat around later in the break room talking with Hollywood about women (and my lack of one), the film industry, and anything under the sun. Jackknife came in and could talk with Hollywood in such a personal way that I never could. I'm just not the kind of person who can say 'fuck you' to anybody I care about, even in jest. It just doesn't sound good and there are more articulate and amusing ways to tell somebody to go get screwed, but Jack was a different kind of guy and he could pull that off. But again, just not the words I would choose.

There is rarely a conversation in that break room that I have been in on where the memory of the killed escort doesn't come up. By no means callus or insensitive, Jack asked Hollywood when the guy got 'whacked'. Fortunately, it was almost ten years ago, in that it happens so rarely. I didn't even know the guy, but I really felt for him and his family. He got wailed because of some driver's carelessness, selfishness, whatever, take your pick. The reason was the most common of all, 'I didn't see him'. I've always said that traffic accidents are the result of people being stupid, selfish, arrogant, and lots of other negative attributes, but it's a tragedy when an innocent person pays the ultimate price for it, which is why you have to be hyper-vigilant on the road, especially on a bike. And sometimes, even that's not enough.

 **RIDE 17**

I t was just me and Snapshot on a single ride. I was feeling sluggish and slow, speaking quietly with a 'don't rush me' attitude. I only got in one cup of coffee before we had to take off.

At the service, there was a woman around thirty some years old, dressed in black felt high heels, a tight black dress and some silky black top that made her unbelievably sexy; in fact, too sexy I thought. This wouldn't be the last time I'd see attractive women at funerals who seemed to have lost sight of the purpose of the event. It shouldn't be viewed as an opportunity to be the most alluring person there, like it's some kind of competition. The running wisdom is to be keenly aware of the family's sense of loss and dress conservatively for the service, not shine a spotlight on yourself to the point of distraction.

Shortly into the run, the bike would die on me when I would reach an intersection. I could tell it wasn't a fuse because I could get it back in neutral and start it up again. It died about three times in a row, but got it going again and took off to the next intersection, revving the engine at 4000 rpms just to keep it running. I mean, *goddamn* these bikes were plagued with problems. I made it to the cemetery without further incident, the strange problem passing like a case of hiccups. Snapshot reached the top of a hill and then *his* bike died on him. It was unbelievable, yet totally within normal expectations. He started rolling the bike down the hill to get up some speed and popped it into gear, getting the bike running again with an easy compression start. Fingers crossed, we could only hope to limp these trouble-prone bikes back to the shop without any further problems.

We cruised along the roads and highways at a leisurely pace, taking in the beauty of the season. He was glad to be off duty and on his way to a nine day vacation in Reno. Me on the other hand, vacations were just a dream. I couldn't pay the rent. It was a sunny day and there were people everywhere in a general good mood. And the people are waving when they saw us rolling by. A nice mother points at us for her child and I wave to the critter. On the highway, motorcyclists, especially Harley riders, tend to give a friendly hand sign of some kind. Kids are staring out the windows of a mini van I'm passing, cute girls waving and walking across an overpass. I love it. That's as good as it gets.

 **RIDE 18 = 19**

B oth rides would be just me and Jackknife on a cool cloudy Monday. He told me to follow him to the nearby garage of the so-called motorcycle escort competition, Jawbone. I'd never met him before and had only heard about him in regard to the reckless nature of his company and the inexperience of his riders, lacking riding discipline and sending them out without extensive training. Jawbone didn't do anything resembling evals as far as I knew. Jack had known him for years, gone fishing together, things like that. When I met him, I was the odd man out and things were kind of awkward. I couldn't really get much of a read on him.

While he and Jack did some catching up, I looked over the ten or so motorcycles he had in his possession, all of them nice police bikes, but three of them were Harleys. I oogled over them while Jack and Jawbone talked about going fishing someday before the weather went to hell for the season. Granted, the Harleys didn't look much like what I associate with cop bikes, but what beautiful beasts they were and I wanted to ride one like nobody's business. At that point in my life, I had never ridden a Harley and this was one of those seminal moments where in the back of my head I was saying "I have got to get me one of these some day." -And 15 years later, I would have one.

We left Jawbone's place just in time to make the service getting out at the funeral home, the pallbearers were carrying the coffin out right as we pulled up. Jack knew we were rushed and stepped up to the crowd with the orange funeral papers in hand. "Anybody who is going on to the cemetery, would you please take one of these stickers, place it in your window and turn on your headlights, please." We handed out a dozen or so papers and were off. I had no idea where we were going through the route, even though I had been over the best course estimation with Hollywood before Jack even got there. At one point during the procession when the radios weren't working as usual, we were yelling at each other to be heard on a four lane highway. As to my hearing ability he shouted with a smile, "You are the worst! The worst!"

I knew it wouldn't be amusing in his mind for long.

WAITING for the second service to finish, there was Golf, the funeral director I had met before at the Mormon service. He did these hearse runs more often than I did motorcycle rides. He lived in a room above the funeral home, an old, almost gothic place. Jack said it was one of the coolest places for a funeral director to live at. Golf had a great sense of humor but was a real wise ass, as one person said of him to his face, 'You only know how to joke through slamming and insulting people'. Which may have been true, but it worked.

We waited downstairs in a tiny room, people in suits coming and going, standing in the door and leaving shortly thereafter, until a young face came along and said that everybody was already in their cars. WHAT?! This was unheard of, and we ran upstairs, handed out the papers and rolled out of there without any discussion of the plan or the route.

A few times Jackknife would stop at a busy intersection and prop the bike on the kickstand, waving me by. He would say, "Go get the next one."

I would speed away not knowing where the next light was or which direction to take it. We got through it alright, delivering the procession to Willamette National just like the first run, but trading roles in what places to hold at the end. Finished the ride smooth as could be, the cars slowly turning into the entrance in a peaceful, orderly formation. It was picture perfect, but I think that was just down to sheer luck. A lack of planning is never a good thing and eventually your luck runs out.

RIDE 20

Yesterday was the double header with Jackknife. Today we would just have a single ride. I had been looking forward to crossing this point for a long time and it was finally here. To the company, ride 20 meant nothing, but to me, it was a lot. I was just glad I was able to get in that many rides before the weather went to crap or I got let go or was forced to work at some dead end, low-paying job, which was what I had become accustomed to.

Getting out to the service was great, the lane changes were smooth, the communication was good at first, our parallel tandem riding was clean and precise. On the way out there, Jack tried to get hold of me three times over the radio but I didn't hear a thing because I had rigged some Sony Walkman earphones in my walkie-talkie. They had a frayed cord though, so the sound was hit and miss at best, no better than the headset I checked out at the garage. So I plugged in the old, standard headset and it sounded like crap before we even got to the church.

As usual, the route that seemed to be apparent at the

garage would be completely changed once we arrived at the service and talked to the funeral director and driver. The funeral papers were handed out, the cars got ready, the red swirling light on the dash of the hearse was flashing. Everyone was ready to go, with the exception of me.

There was some confusion on my part about where the cars would be coming out of the parking lot into the road. Jack had just told me they would be coming out one way, and not a second goes by and he tells the hearse driver the complete opposite. I asked Jack if I misunderstood and he got pretty upset. This was a first. He bit my head off big time, reiterating what he had just told me, this time in the most condescending, scolding tone of voice and then took off. I'm sure I sounded pesky, but that's what I got for asking too many questions. It was all uphill from there, any fun that could have been had was in the wind.

I held the oncoming traffic of one lane as the cars of the procession slowly pulled out. They always come out too slow and non-uniformly, just agonizingly time-consuming. Then there was a car without a sticker and no lights on and I was waving it out so we could get under way. I realized two seconds too late that it didn't want to be part of the procession and Jack was angrily waving for me to get on my bike and get rolling. I cruised down the hill past the cars and the hearse, leading them into the hairiest intersection of the entire trip. Jack was holding the traffic up ahead, turning us in a direction that yet again contradicted the plan, but I didn't hear anything over the radio. He waved me on and yelled what I thought sounded like, "You got a problem with that?!" -Which wasn't actually what he said at all, but something to that effect. I rode to a car length in front of the hearse and slowed down, waiting to be informed.

We got through the hardest part, then Jack's bike suddenly

blew a coil on the second turn of the route, instantly cutting his four cylinder engine down in half, barely working. Seemed like everything was going wrong, yet we managed to get the procession to the cemetery without much further incident. But it was *not* a good ride.

After looking over his bike and being as perplexed as I was, he gave me a stern warning that I needed to show progress at a far greater rate or I would be let go; in other words, fired for not being good enough, not up to speed.

He said, "I can see why Hollywood gets frustrated with you." His suggestions to improve were that I would have to hear what was going over the radio, be in contact, (despite the crappy headsets that I couldn't hear a word over) and that I would have to know the tri-county area better than a cab driver. Self-defeating thoughts ran rampant through my mind, worst of all being that I would be fired from the single job that I loved the most to date because I was too stupid or not good enough. It was a nightmare suddenly made very real. Talk about unemployed.

"The truth is the truth." I said, and Jack agreed, knowing I understood the gravity of the situation. I told him the same thing I told Hollywood, who explained his concerns and reservations about me on the same subjects. I told them that I was giving it my best, that I wasn't holding anything back. To be let go from something so important to you, despite giving it your best, is a crushing feeling, no matter how old or young you are.

From River View Cemetery we managed to get back to the garage without the bike going completely tits up. In the last hundred yards of the approach, Jack said he could limp it over to Portland Kawasaki for a diagnostic and veered off.

When I got back to the garage, I was never more motivated to leave as soon as possible. I checked all my stuff back in, cleaned out my coffee mug, took off the badge and everything else. Then Hollywood and Hump pulled in just as I was ready to go and I overheard how they had run into a maniacal motorist on their run. I went to the break room to find out what happened. During his procession, Hump came across a car that had no regard for the law, despite somebody being on a cop motorcycle with flashing red lights. Hollywood took down all the information about the incident, not having witnessed it, along with the license plate. He would call it in and somebody, as in the police, would have a talk with the driver, a warning, and that would be the end of it.

Jack popped in the break room from the Kawasaki shop and explained the bike's problem. Once again, it was a cheap part the could easily crap out and affect the performance of the bike in a big way. No mention was made there at the table about the earlier communication problems we had, but without a doubt I knew Hollywood would hear about it at length and it would serve to solidify their doubts about me. And now was not the time to bring up how Jack had given two conflicting instructions earlier in the day. Or maybe it was… but I didn't say anything.

I also made no mention that I was glad to have my 20th ride under my belt, but it had largely been a step back in the eyes of Jack. In his mind, I wasn't grasping notions that should have been common sense.

Hollywood said that at long last he had found a nickname for me. Even the secretary in earshot paused and waited, everyone held their breath, there was a stillness in the air. I think the coffee pot even stopped percolating for a few seconds.

"Oh no." I said, laughing, knowing I would have to live with whatever it might be, no options or multiple choice. Then he declared me

"MIGHTY MOUSE"

-A pint-sized cartoon character famous for flying into a

situation singing, "Here I come to save the daaaay!" wearing generic yellow and red tights with a cape. A peal of laughter tore through the room. Before I could ask Hollywood exactly what it meant or the significance of it, he left to call in the plate on the reckless driver and we all left. But my new name was now set in stone.

 **RIDE 21**

Once again, the next day was a single ride with Jack. At this point, I was trying to think of things I could do to improve my ability to know the best routes from funeral homes to cemeteries, but studying two dimensional maps in a Thomas Guide just seemed asinine. My big concern was that I was never going to get to know Portland and all the important streets of the surrounding cities fast enough for them to send me out on my own, which was the level I needed to be at.

It was a really early ride and as usual, I was there at the garage way before I needed to be there. Got everything ready in a slow, removed state of mind. It was as if, in my mind, the honeymoon was over. Hollywood and Hump pulled into the garage and I barely said a word. Felt like I had a rock over me I didn't want to crawl out from under.

Rolling on the streets on the way to the service, for the first time the radio communication was perfect. I heard everything absolutely clear. -And I have no idea why, only know that the radio gods were smiling on me that day. Just like the day before, the plan of the procession pulling out of the parking lot was changed at the last minute. I asked in relatively the same way as I had yesterday to confirm the alteration, but no blowback this time. Maybe somebody got up on the right side of the bed this morning.

While the service was getting out and families were being reunited, the people were usually surprised to see motorcycle cops at the door. It's during this brief window of time when I see all these new faces; most are ordinary, average, some of them ugly, and then there are the very few women which are utterly beautiful and impossible to ignore. Split second glances are shared, filled with volumes of meaning, like in slow motion, we imagine if things were different. Could I, could she, be in a happier place than we are now? Could we escape our present condition to some place more... heavenly, closer to the dreams we have? Or per chance we could go back in time and make different life choices and entertain the notion of what if...? And as quickly as the moment of connection happens, it passes; reality comes back to remind us of where we are in the journey, to embrace us, to constrict us, to let us know we are on *this* path and the river is taking us in that direction, not another.

There were about thirty cars in the procession, but we were going to try to make it a milk run, just a low-key, slow ride to the cemetery without getting an uptight driver's shorts in a knot.

There was great communication on the part of Jackknife telling me the intention of the next intersection, and for the first time I could hear it all and respond that I understood instead of asking to repeat. I was leading the way to the last intersection before the cemetery hill and Jack says over the radio, "Alright, this next light is a right turn on Yosemite." It didn't make sense. The cemetery was at the top of the hill, but I figured he knew what he was doing, some kind of back road or something. I wasn't going to question him twice with everybody listening, including Hollywood and Hump across town on the radios.

The funeral director came over the walkie-talkie, "Jack, you know we're going to Lincoln, right?" And Thank God for it.

"Oh, I'm sorry!" Jack said back. "I was thinking of my second service, just off Yosemite."

His next words clearly for me, he said "Sorry. Hold the intersection and I'll take 'em up the hill."

"Copy that." I replied. "I was wondering why you were suggesting the scenic route."

I held the last traffic light, Jack pulling up to the right side of the lane and telling me to move forward so he could get his bike out of the way of antsy traffic wanting to go. We got up to the top of the hill and delivered the procession to the grounds. For him, it was just one of hundreds of rides he'd done over the years, but for me, every one counted.

Just as we were rolling the last two blocks to the garage, Jack said, "I think you're ready for your first solo ride." -Which came as a total surprise.

"That's a far cry from yesterday." I said.

He called over the radio to the office and Hollywood, "5-7 to dispatch, have arrived back at the garage and will be taking 5-4 to Portland Kawasaki. Mighty Mouse did awesome."

18

EVALS 2

Another Sunday spent riding the police bikes around in a parking lot, pushing everybody's individual envelope. This time we weren't being graded, scored or timed, it was simply meant as a rust remover and polishing session. Some of the same maneuvers that I had trouble with on the last eval would be there again and just as formidable.

I remember on the first eval, where I rode to the parking lot on my own bike, I was envious of the guys who got to ride the police bikes out there. This time it was my job to the ride one of them out there, in plain clothes. If you think the public looks at you funny during a procession, they really look perplexed when they see four guys riding police bikes in formation with different helmets, leather, nothing the same about any of us.

There was a new guy there, far less senior than me, I believe around my age, but even he had been riding a year and a half longer than I had. He had done one or two rides for the company and was still considered a break in. He had the exact same kind of street helmet I did, even the dark visor, which he wore while on the cop bikes, on the road and on the course. I remember the guys telling me when I wore my helmet on the course, it limited my vision, but I didn't think so. My peripheral vision was just fine, you're either looking through the turn or you're not. I wore one of their helmets when somebody would let me get on the bike.

The course consisted of about eight cones in a line, not so far apart, the serpentine part, where you weave between them, a lot of clutch, rear brake and thrusts of the throttle. It was the easiest part for me and I would never knock over cones in this part, it was the other stuff and tight turns at slow speed that I had trouble with. The four of us rode through the maze, the new guy must have dumped the bike at least five times, and like me before, they had to show him the best way to pick it up. Now, I had no fear of dumping the bike and expected to do so. Ironically, I think I was the only one not to dump a bike that day with the exception of Hollywood. Even Jackknife and Hump dumped theirs once or twice. You had to watch out for gas on the pavement where we were expected to make a turn.

I must have rode about forty miles going through that parking lot before getting off the bike. Everyone else had been sitting on the side well before I wanted to stop practicing. I wondered if I was holding them up from something. I had the serpentine down cold, and just worked on the particular points I was having trouble with. Finally, I started getting through the second turn that was the toughest for me. I had it, knew I could do it, and do it again to show that it wasn't a fluke.

HOLLYWOOD WASN'T there to see me get this stuff and do it right. As a police reservist, he had to check out some alarm that had gone off somewhere across town. When he came back, he changed the course slightly by moving the cones in and making the turns tighter, making some maneuvers completely out of reach for my skill level. To watch somebody pull it off, showing that it could be done, was to see expert riding at its best.

For later review, as usual, the rides were being taped for further evaluation. As they were shooting, Hollywood checked what he was recording over and nearly erased a copy of his three minute reel of all kinds of stunts he had been involved in. There were lots of explosions, cars being catapulted from ramps at 70 miles an hour, in arenas with full capacity crowds, cars jumped into rivers (and the ocean), motorcycle stunts, he drove the General Lee in The Dukes of Hazzard for three years. There were stunts unlike anything I'd ever seen, such as three cars in a row, propped to stand up on their bumpers, then he hurtles in a car and smashes through them like they're dominos. He held a Guinness world record for one of his stunts for about six months, but record breaking was not what possessed him to do it. He even played Jason in one of the Friday the 13th movies, wearing a hockey mask and getting plowed over by a car like a rag doll. And it was *hilarious*.

It almost seems to boggle the mind why anybody would put themselves through these highly dangerous rigors and challenges, but damn it looks fun! To be the faceless guy who hurtles a car like a rocket through the back of three exploding buses is just the kind of thing I would like to get paid for doing, or just getting paid to do it would be the icing on the cake. It's the same principle with the motorcycle escorts, nobody realistically does it for the money, it's fun, you get the memories of a lifetime, and enough to buy a couple beers at the end of the day.

I WAS HAVING trouble with the same thing; a slow hard-leaning turn left, scraping the running boards, get it back up straight, then a hard right in a slower turn without knocking over any cones. Once again, the first turn wasn't a problem, came into the approach in the right place at the right speed, but would lose my inertia. I would come out of the turn too wide, go off into uncharted waters like a bull in a china shop, sometimes riding over three or so cones at a forty five degree angle. It's not fun. In a right slow turn like that, you really have to rip the throttle to get out of it or you'll dump it.

At least this time I was keeping my cool, laughing it off and coming back around for another try as soon as they reset the cones like pinsetters in a bowling alley. I would see them walking back to the island in the lot and I would say, "Don't sit down just yet." Within a pass or two I would take out three or four cones, maybe drag one under the engine halfway across the lot. Everybody else was pretty much done and off their bikes, but Hollywood wasn't going to let me off easy without getting this second turn.

"We're not leaving until you get this." he said.

There I was, holding up class as it were, and it wasn't looking like I was going to get it anytime soon, despite the best advice. At this point I was really tired, worn out, and completely frustrated. I kept blowing the second turn and wanted to get out of there. I really didn't want to be the focus of a lecture if I couldn't get this before I ran out of gas or something. It was getting really shitty gas mileage working through the course and the tank was running low. Finally, I got it and knew I had it, just like you know when the bat connects with the ball that you've hit a home run. I went back to try and prove that it wasn't a fluke, but didn't get it as good. Oh well I figured. If I'd learned anything, it was not to knock myself out too much about not getting something the first time around. There'll be other chances.

Back at the garage, I was complimented by Jackknife and

Hump about the progress I'd shown. I think Hump was genuinely impressed by my rate of improvement. I had been riding for just over a year now, but was doing things people riding a decade couldn't do.

Hollywood showing how it's done

19

RIDE 22

Late August and Oregon's usually sublime summer weather was getting to be a bit much. I had been working six days a week for my construction company for the last two and a half weeks, which was quite the contrast to how things had been going over the last month or two. I was making good money from a lot of overtime, but I was really itching to get a ride in to keep up with my progress, keep the momentum going. I needed a ride like a junkie needs a fix. It was kind of ironic, after construction work being so hit and miss for months, now I was too busy for the escort work and was afraid that if I didn't get in a ride soon, Hollywood was going to cut me loose until I had a lot more free time on my hands.

Was at the garage crazy early as usual, because why not? Did I have some great girlfriend or wife laying in bed beside me saying "Oh, don't go! Stay with me a little longer…" (?) No, I most assuredly did not. So why not get out of my Fortress of Solitude a little earlier than needed?

Did all the pre-run checks on the bike, but later realized I forgot to lube the chain, one of the most important things to

do. I knew I'd forgotten something, and told myself I'd deal
with it when I got back.

For the first time in a long time, I saw one of the three guys
that was hired the same time as me. Just like my situation, he
had to pursue some job that could pay the rent and had been
employed on and off by a pool cleaning company. I mean seriously, a pool cleaning business, in Oregon? How stable could
that work be? Unsurprisingly, business was slow and he had a
good deal of time for rides lately, so here he was. He had cut
his hair real short, like buzz cut short and as a result, earned
himself a new nickname: Fuzz.

We talked about this and that, catching up. I said that I
couldn't wait to be sent out on my first solo ride. He laughed
and said, "I sure wouldn't expect that for at least a year." He
didn't mean that as an insult, and went on to say, "They
aren't going to send one of us out alone until we know the
route backwards and forwards before we do it. They would
have to have a lot more confidence in us than they've got
now, no matter how well we ride." He hadn't been sent out
solo either, but at least they consistently had him leapfrog-
ging, one step closer to handling rides on your own, whereas
Hollywood wanted me to continue bumping for the experience. I mentioned Jackknife's comment about me being ready
for a solo run and he didn't know what to make of it, but
Fuzz was quite positive that such a ride wasn't in my foresee-
able future.

Hollywood and I jumped on the bikes to get gas, filled up
and headed down a couple highways to get to the North Portland service being held at a Black church. It was in an especially bad part of town, gang members and shifty-looking
people were riding in the streets and sidewalks on overly small
pedal bikes, young guys hanging around on street corners,
getting into Cadillacs as they would stop to talk and let
someone jump in back. Like so many troubled hoods, every-

body seemed to fit into one of two categories; those looking to get into trouble and those trying to stay out of it.

While waiting for the service to get out, Hollywood and I had a lot of time to talk about all kinds of things. I would often just keep my mouth shut because whenever I seemed to open it, I'd just put my foot in it and say something stupid. However, I did finally learn the origin and meaning of my nickname 'Mighty Mouse', which was largely for the reason I had thought. As it turns out, one time when I was a fledgling rider filling up at the Texaco station with Hollywood, some joker of a gas pumper shared an observation about me. The guy had probably seen every new rider ever since he started working there. Seemed like he was *always* there. Early on, he saw me pushing my bike around on my tiptoes, ever so carefully trying to get it near the right gas pump.

"Man, look at him trying to get that thing around. He's really a small one. Kinda like Mighty Mouse."

And there it was.

I found out that the one rider less senior than me had received a nickname already, even though I'm sure he had less than five rides under his belt. Hollywood based the name on what he saw the guy do on the second round of evals. He called him 'Slump', because of the way he slumped into the handlebars, kind of slouching or drooping. Sounds like the same thing that Hollywood told me not to do after about ride 6. Let me tell you, 'Slump' was just the kind of nickname I was hoping *not* to get. I was afraid of being called 'Dumper' or something for tipping the bike over on the first time out.

Hollywood told me that while I was gone all those days doing construction work, Snapshot had retired from doing the cemetery runs. It wasn't hard to fathom, as the expert rider he was, after having as many close calls and a recent crash, for so little pay, the reward didn't come anywhere near the risk involved. I was young, struggling for anything and everything. I was doing it for the thrill of it and other aspects. The pay meant nothing, but was helpful, whereas Snapshot was already a full time cop and this was something he did on the side because he was needed. As far as I knew, my ride with him before his vacation was his last one. He must have seriously thought about it and made up his mind in Reno.

Hollywood and I waited outside the church, overhearing what sounded like a Holy Rollers service, what with all the wailing that was going on inside. Some singing, a little sermon, a little more singing, it sounded great, but it just kept going on and on. We had so much time to burn, we met with the funeral director, the hearse driver, all the head guys involved, just waiting to get the show on the road. Nothing rushed about this run.

The funeral director was utterly notorious for being a bad client. The people in his processions consistently didn't listen to or completely ignored directions about how the driving event was supposed to go down. I was told that in past processions, if there wasn't a police bike to secure an intersection at a red light, the hearse would just barrel through it as if all the cross traffic would come to a screeching halt at the sight of a hearse with a red swirling light. I could envision the chaos it would cause, like some Blues Brothers chase scene with huge car pile-ups, one car T-boning another and then another, window glass exploding in the air, a chain reaction of mayhem, while the hearse driver continues on, completely oblivious and uncaring.

Hollywood kept checking his watch, waiting for the service to get out, but it never seemed to come. He wrestled with the idea of taking off so he could reach his second service in time and someone could meet him out there. What gave him pause was the thought of leaving me to handle this ride that he knew probably wouldn't go well, if this client's history was any indication. I tried to reassure him that I was ready for such a simple, straightforward solo run. If everybody went by the rules, namely the hearse driver, everything should be fine. I think he knew that was not in the cards. He held out on deciding for about half an hour, consulting the office and other riders, including Jackknife, who was driving a limo across town somewhere, but no great solution was revealing itself.

Reluctantly, Hollywood had to take off to the second service to meet up with Kickstand, who was already heading out there. So there I was, hours ago being told that my first solo run would be a year off, and now it was go time. I was psyched and a bit nervous, knowing this would be the opposite of an easy run and that it more than likely would turn into a shit-show. It's no accident the people in this funeral director's processions had a reputation as a notorious crowd, wanting to use us to help them with their needs, but resentful of the presence of a caucasian authority figure; basically white cops. About ten minutes after Hollywood had split, I saw the hearse driver again and explained to him that the service had gone longer than anticipated, forcing Hollywood to jet off to the next one. He took it rather well, but I could see he wasn't thrilled about the news. They had paid for two bikes and three hours of our time, but our guys estimated the service wouldn't take more than an hour, and when it took two, we were screwed.

I could see the coffin being carried down the exit stairway and held the door open, something that for some reason, nobody else was thinking of doing. It was called being considerate. Some people saw me holding the door open with the orange funeral papers in hand and would quietly ask for them. More quiet than their request, I would lean towards their ears and politely say, "Just put it on the dashboard and turn on your lights when we get rolling, please." They would usually nod and walk out to the sidewalk, saying hellos and goodbyes to familiar faces.

As things got rolling in the parking lot, I was taking extra precautions to see that all went well. As the cars started pulling into the street, I made sure they had their lights on as best I could and got with the program. I told the lead driver specifically that if he came to a red light and I wasn't there, that he should not even consider going through it. He conveyed that he understood this completely, although I had been warned that their understanding ways meant nothing once they hit the road.

I did a radio check with the driver and he didn't respond. I heard that the three guys in the hearse always did nothing but talk on the way to the cemetery, not paying attention to any direction changes or instructions. I got the impression they went out of their way to make things difficult so they could turn around and blame us later. I hit my pursuit lights and swirling red, came over the radio to anyone listening, "Alright, driver; whenever you're ready."

He started to move forward and I had to remind him, as he was driving a hearse from my company, "Be sure to hit your red light."

He flipped on the red swirling light on the dashboard and came to the intersection, slowly leading the procession to the first and only real turn of the ride. It was a single left and the rest would be holding intersections on the same street all the way to the last turn into the cemetery, about three miles away. The only problem was that there were about 40 to 50 cars, far more than I had handed out papers for, meaning that many of the cars who intended to stay with the procession would be unidentified. Who was the last car? Who knew? -But we were rolling now and I had to wing it.

I held the intersection on a slow neighborhood street into that first turn, and it was then that I realized I really had a huge procession for a single person, even for two riders. The cars with their lights on just kept coming and coming and coming, and too slowly. They would get bunched up and stopped because the first light up ahead was red, so I jumped on the bike, cut through the line of traffic and held up the intersection, waving our cars through, blowing the whistle full blare.

The next light was only a block away and rightly so, the hearse stopped because it too was red. The procession was bumper to bumper again, stopping all the way back in the middle of my intersection behind them. What a freaking mess, right out of the gate. The cross traffic light went green against the procession, but no one could move, like a stalemate. The way things should have gone, Hollywood would have been at the next light, getting those cars moving, but here I was in the back, kind of behind the eight ball.

I can only imagine the confusion going through the minds of drivers seeing this. Right from the get go, the problems I faced weren't from the public and cross traffic on the streets; it was from the jackasses in the procession who seemed like they were going out of their way to mess things up. At the second light up ahead, while waiting for the light to turn green in our favor, the people in the third car, behind the limo, the driver and passenger got out of their car to talk to the driver of the car behind them. Remember, this is way before everybody had a cell phone, smart phone, whatever, so if you wanted to talk to somebody in another car while driving, you stopped in the middle of an intersection, got out of your car and talked face to face. To hell with everybody else. So the light goes green, the hearse and limo drive off, the people of the third car not having a clue because they're busy dealing with the people behind them. I can see all of this unfold from a block away. The cars at the next intersection are wondering what the hell is going on and so was I, so stupid it was comical, but nothing funny about it. I cranked the throttle of my standing bike a couple times like I'm screaming towards them, which got their attention and they realize the hearse has gone (and that they're complete idiots). They get in their car and slowly take off, now huge holes in the procession and the timing completely screwed.

I'm still at the first light, watching this fiasco unfold from a distance. Ok, enough of this getting people on the road, I had to be at that next intersection and get things sorted out. I ride up to the second intersection and secure it, leaning the bike on the kickstand again and stepping away, into clear view for all to see. I make a point to get everybody's attention, and I mean absolutely everybody. I'm standing in the middle of what should be a busy intersection, with a procession of angry cars passing me by, concerned that if anybody does anything out of line that endangers me, their ass is mine. I'm a civilian. I don't have to worry about being bounced off a police force in disgrace for flipping out on somebody who nearly kills me. Strangely enough, the public was surprisingly agreeable. Even Tri-Met buses, the most zealous behemoths of the tri-county roads, were moving out of the way or stopping when they would first catch sight of me. I would wave my thanks or give a thumbs up or something to show my appreciation.

Block by block, the procession was held up, waiting, with some windows rolled down in the summer heat. Some guys had the nerve to say that I wasn't doing my job because the procession just wasn't flowing gracefully through lights non-stop. As people slowly drove by me standing in one intersection or another, a few were trying to convince me of what a lousy job I was doing, which couldn't have been further from the truth. One guy said, "Hey, we're getting separated, man. You should do your job better."

What the guy deserved to hear in response was: "Hey, fuck off man. If you have some way I can be in five places at once, you let me know Einstein." But I couldn't say that. I can here though. Instead, I refrained enough to say, "I'm only one person and can only be in one place at one time."

The fantastically wise and insightful people in that car didn't like that answer, apparently not impressed by my incredibly precise and ballsy throttling up to the front, skirting between oncoming traffic and the cars in the procession, making little or no effort to help me get ahead of the hearse by them moving over to the right and out of the way.

All kinds of cars were getting into the procession that had no idea or didn't care what was going on. Bogies. They didn't have their lights on and would *stop* at a red light, despite the fact I was standing there waving them through. They don't have a clue a funeral procession is going on. They don't know what they've gotten into. Every single intersection was taking a couple minutes, more chances for cars to inadvertently get into the mess. Time seemed to drag on and slow down, seconds felt like minutes. So much could go wrong, dozens of cars in every direction, all wanting to go, lots of confusion to go around. But there wasn't any honking, yelling, or sounds of crashing metal and shattering glass, which was about all I could hope for in this situation. Just get everybody to the cemetery in one piece with no damage and it's a win.

Soon, the end was in sight. I was going to pull it off. I could see the green fences of Rose City Cemetery and the hearse a quarter mile ahead. There was no way I could get ahead before it made the final left turn into the grounds. It was on its own. But a sense of relief came over me as I rode in the oncoming traffic lane to the left of the procession. I desperately needed to cut to the outside right, the passenger side of the cars, so I could jam up ahead and hold the oncoming traffic against the final left turn into the cemetery. I saw a small window of opportunity of a space between some cars before they could bunch up again, but then I saw a police motorcycle up ahead with lights flashing at the final turn, directing them into the grounds.

In a split second, the opportunity to cut right disappeared

as the cars were bumper to bumper again, oncoming traffic made an escape to the left impossible. I hit the brakes hard, locking up into a rear tire skid until I was sliding sideways at a 45 degree angle. I didn't panic, but eased off, and the bike corrected, jumped straight back up. I went around the right side of the stopped car without touching it. I didn't make eye contact with the driver, but I turned my head around and threw up my hand as if to say, 'Did you see that?! That was for you! Now I'm off!' It was a good ten foot skid, sliding into a potential dumper, definitely the hairiest skid I'd ever pulled off up to then.

Sure enough, there was Jackknife holding the final turn into the cemetery, completely out of uniform. He clearly had jumped from his limo at the garage onto a bike, throwing on only a helmet and leather. He was still wearing green pants and checkered argyle socks. I rode up and stood my bike next to his and we shook hands. He thought I did great under the circumstances. As the procession turned into the cemetery grounds, I didn't see a satisfied, content face among them. What can I say? -They were a bunch of unappreciative losers, extremely upset when they learned there was only one bike when they had paid for two. They didn't convey this before taking off, but instead, during the procession, showed their displeasure by being a caravan of jackasses. Some of them even called Hollywood's cell number, a very privileged direct line, because the funeral director had given it to them and raised all hell about the run.

LATER THAT DAY back at the garage, Hollywood and I sat down to talk about the run, and after I told him about the positive learning experience I felt I'd gained, he informed me of the client's pissing and moaning. He told me that they were first and foremost upset that there was only one rider when they had paid for two, and one had the nerve to say that 'The guy who got us there didn't know what he was doing.' I think this was said because, in jest, Hollywood introduced me as a new rider and someone to be careful of, which I can clearly see how they played on that to their best advantage; just assholes.

Like taking the wind out of my sails, Hollywood said it was unfortunate that I had been put in such a situation, saying I wasn't ready for my first solo ride, even after what I felt I had just done had proved that I was. He wasn't there to see it for himself, only heard from a litany of natural born complainers, and if that's how I handled a procession where everyone was working against you, imagine how things would have been if everything had been going well. But I have to take my lumps like everyone else and at the end of the day, I did have my first solo run and no one could take it from me.

It turns out that because of that one day and not being available for construction work, it was the straw that broke the camel's back. My brother in law Brick was telling my immediate boss that I should be available for flagging work every day of the week. This escort work had caused them headaches enough times that things had reached a breaking point.

20

RIDE 23

The next ride was a month later to the day. The construction work scheduling bullshit had been driving me crazy. I was seeing less and less work on a weekly basis and my construction work dissatisfaction was a constant gripe. At one point, Brick threatened to fire me if the escort work ever interfered with the crazy ass constant rescheduling of the construction projects. Because I hadn't called O.F.S. on Saturday to say I wasn't available, they had me down for a ride Monday morning. Brick was pissed when I told him about the misunderstanding and he snapped like a dry twig.

"You should tell those guys to fuck off. They can handle it without you," he said. I pleaded with him to do this one last ride, then I would square away with O.F.S. and tell Hollywood that I wouldn't be available until the construction company wouldn't need me for a while. But Brick was having none of it. As a flagger, I was the least of his concerns, down at the bottom of the food chain, and here I was being a big pain in the ass. He said, "If you aren't out at the job site at 7 tomorrow morning, you can tell those guys you'll be a full time rider." Click. He hung up on me. That was new. This is my brother in law and the closest thing to a brother I've ever had. That's a day I won't soon forget. I knew I had to drop that construction job, find something better, and never look back.

I had to call the O.F.S. answering service and they desperately managed to get through to Kickstand at home on a Sunday night. He managed to call me back right away. The schedule for Monday at O.F.S. was the busiest I had ever heard and the longest message by far. They had all the bikes and limos going out, jumping across town to here and there all day. They were so hard pressed that they were using three different Jawbone riders to pull off the rides. It was easy to see they were up shit creek if they were using Jawbone riders and me, without them knowing if I was really 100% available or not.

Kickstand was very understanding and sympathetic to my plight. I apologized profusely. I didn't want to be labeled a pain in the ass by them too. He told me that it was alright, they would find some way to cover for me. But he urged me to tell them when they count on me to be available again. All I could tell him was… November; months away. That's how long Brick told me he could keep me employed through. Now here I was, having worked two construction days in the last two weeks and I was pissed. It was always one day to the next. I would wait for a call that never came to tell me what the hell was going on. And trying to get hold of people in the construction business can be a real bitch sometimes. It doesn't matter that they have pagers or early model cell phones. I couldn't get a hold of Brick or any other foreman to find out what was up.

After a week and a half of virtual unemployment, that Wednesday I was so pissed off I called O.F.S. and told the secretary that I would be available tomorrow, Friday, and Saturday. Ten days and just one of construction work, and literally not five minutes go by until my phone rings and Brick says, "Steve-O, you're gonna be out in Hillsboro tomorrow. Be there at 7." Dollars to donuts, it fucking figured. What can I say? I had to call the secretary back seven minutes after talking to her and cancel my availability for the next day. How could I not have appeared like more trouble than I was worth?

WHEN O.F.S. WAS STRETCHED TOO thin for available riders, they would throw the extra gigs to Jawbone and his riders like scraps off a table. Jawbone was only too happy to have the business. His outfit didn't have the best of reputations. I asked Hump what he thought about the Jawbone riders he'd dealt with. He said, "They're scary, man. Keep your eyes *wide* open. One of those guys just about ran me off the road." Their reputation was notorious, as always. I'd never heard a good word about them.

I had worked four construction days that week and had just got home on a hot, Friday afternoon when my phone rang before I could get out of my sweat-soaked clothes. Kickstand was asking if I was available for Saturday. My mom and I understood that I was to be working with dad and her to pull out their dead raspberry bushes on Saturday. I told Kickstand that I could swing it and he put me on the schedule. I squared it away with the folks, but it was a bummer not being in on their 'big dig' because my dad's back was killing him.

I got to the garage way early as usual, and saw Fuzz (aka The Pool Boy), one of the guys who was hired at the same time as me. I was told that his name had been changed yet again from Fuzz, as a result of his insanely short haircut, to Soda Pop, because during one procession, he ran over a half-empty pop can in the street which exploded all over Hump and the lady in the car next to him. I was told that by the time Hump got back to the garage, he was so sticky, he felt like he'd been dipped in molasses.

· · ·

HUSKY WAS NOW A RETIRED Washington motorcycle cop, and the best rider I'd ever seen with my own eyes, next to Hollywood. He was the perfect example of a true pro who did this kind of work not for the money (there was none to be made), but to fill a need and answer a call. This was the first ride I would have with him and I sure as hell didn't want to leave a bad impression. If it's a bad first ride, it's a hard impression to shake off. Some riders didn't want to ride with me after their initial experience and I didn't want to let Husky down, much less upset him.

My black work boots had a quarter inch of asphalt caked on the bottom from my construction work and it was like having ice under your feet. That's not good when you come to a stop and hold the bike up, standing on your toes and there's nothing there. I got a screwdriver and worked up a sweat getting the sticky black rock off the soles. Husky arrived just as I got the last of it off. No surprise, he didn't know me shit from shine-ola. He told me his name and I said, "I know. I saw you at evals before you retired."

The plan was to meet a Jawbone rider at the service. Husky wasn't going to use a radio, knowing the Jawbone rider wouldn't have one either. It was just further testament to Husky's ability and experience; not needing a walkie talkie to handle things. No radio for me then. Fortunately, the route was simple enough along a single street for a few miles, but with some hairy intersections, the worst of which was one of those massive six way, four lane crossings.

WE RODE in tandem to some degree on the way to the service. I was having trouble at first figuring out his riding style so that I could stay right with him. He would jam through the first three gears like a banshee and then settle in on fourth and get consistent. I was either getting slightly ahead of him or behind, which is no good. It seems like a game of dueling cycles; not really a harmony. At least we had good hand gesture communication. We were great at lane changes, which other riders were more hesitant about and would often stay behind a line of cars or not take advantage of an easy opportunity to avoid being stuck in traffic. With Husky, he would point somewhere up ahead and vroom, we'd take off and get there without a word spoken.

With my last ride being a month ago, I'm sure a lot had transpired while I was away, for what would otherwise be a brief absence at another job. My riding was a little rusty in some ways. At one intersection on the way to the service, I let the clutch out too quickly and killed the bike. Seeing no point in waiting, Husky took off. I restarted it pretty fast and got through the light as it went yellow but I felt pretty stupid. I caught up with him no problem, though I'm sure he was wondering what happened. I was thinking: Grrrr…. Demerits. I was making some beautiful moves and wasn't shaking his confidence, but I wasn't pulling everything off perfectly either. And I was sliding all over the seat because the polyester pants uniform I was wearing was like trying to stay in control on a slip and slide.

As usual, as we rode along, I could point in just about any direction and see some construction project I'd worked on. We drove through an intersection where I spent three months flagging, repaving it, and putting up new traffic lights. At the end of the project, the old street lights were going to be scrapped, so one of the county inspectors and myself took them home. During that time in my Portland apartment life, I had that street light plugged in and the three colors of red, yellow and green would illuminate my otherwise dark room.

When we were making the last turn into the service, we saw the Jawbone rider coming from the other direction and turning into the chapel. To my great surprise, the guy was actually

Jawbone himself. He cruised in on a nice cop Harley that I was dying to ride. I walked up to him and said Hi. This being the first time I'd really had a chance to talk to him, he was very standoffish and his personality left a lot to be desired. I don't know what his deal was, but he had a serious bug up his ass. I had to wonder if he had a chip on his shoulder about something. With two decades of hindsight, what was more likely was that Jackknife had shared his misgivings about me with Jawbone and his attitude was the result. His coat had a Battle Ground, Washington, police badge sewn into it. I never heard that he was any kind of cop, or that any cops would work for him because they all knew of his notorious reputation.

It was a great ride though. We waited for the light to turn green in our favor at a six way intersection, crowded with cars. I gunned to the center of the six-way and set the bike on the stand, holding the traffic. The procession was fairly short for how many cars were in the church parking lot and parked on side streets. It was only about 40 in all. But no great mishaps or headaches and nothing dangerous. Considering Jawbone was in the mix, I chalked it up as a win.

 **RIDE 24**

I t was now mid-October and I had just recently quit my construction job after three and a half years of ups and downs. It was kind of scary and kind of liberating, but not having to be on standby for the construction work freed me up to be available for the escort rides again and some money was better than none. I was also drawing unemployment and that could tide me over until a decent job came up. Or so I hoped.

One new aspect of going back to work for the escort service was that now I had a girlfriend for the first time in about five years. *Five years!* Her name, seriously, was something like Muffin. She liked motorcycles and was the first, and so far, even 25 years later, only passenger on my bike ever. On one of our first dates, we rode to downtown Portland on my crappy Yamaha Virago with a cheap strapless helmet that almost flew off her head as we screamed over the steel grating of a bridge. She had to keep it on her head by holding it with her hand. She had only known me for a week or so, yet had this over-riding trust in my abilities or judgement or something.

. . .

Now THE WEIRD part was that her ex-boyfriend was also a motorcycle rider who supposedly did escorts for funeral services. I mean, what are the odds? Only he did it for the slip shot opposition, claiming to be a Jawbone rider. His crazy ass riding 'style' was enough to keep the girl from getting on the back of his bike permanently. He was what you would call 'accident prone' and other people would call uninsurable. All the pieces of the puzzle of what a loser this guy was were perfectly fitting into place. As if that coincidence wasn't strange enough, she knew Jawbone rather well, because her ex-boyfriends's mother, whom she got along with famously, was actually dating Jawbone at the time. If Portland isn't the smallest big city in America, I'd like to know which one is. There's no seven degrees of separation here; maybe two at best.

The service that day was for a board member of the Tualatin Valley Fire Department; clearly very respected and liked by those that knew him. It was a Catholic affair and during the eulogy I heard something that made an impression on me. The minister said the deceased man saw everything, especially what most people would consider mundane tasks, as an opportunity, even things like mowing the lawn. He said he would see every situation as a new possibility, a new door to open. Doing yardwork was not seen as a backbreaking endeavor, but a chance to get some fresh air and exercise. When they would send him out on some unexpected errand, he would say, "Oh no, don't worry about it. I might see so and so or I might run into what's her name... " It was a positive outlook on life to see nothing but silver linings in everything, a quality I certainly lacked, and naturally, people liked him for it.

This run was a first for me in the sense there was a big red fire truck following us with every attention-grabbing red light swirling and strobe light flashing. You could see us coming from a mile away. Drivers in the oncoming traffic lane, who had no legal reason to stop as we lead the procession, would just about run themselves off the road into the ditch, pulling over as they saw a fireworks show on wheels coming at them at five miles an hour. We were moving at a parade level speed, not like normal, trying to get to the cemetery well under the speed limit. This was a crawl. It wasn't easy leading the pack in first gear the whole time, the bike wanting to stall and cut out because you were barely giving it enough gas to keep going. It was tricky riding of a different kind, utilizing the best of my slow speed skills, a fine balance of clutch and throttle. No racing to the front and securing intersections under pressure, no sirens or horns blaring from the fire truck. Just the familiar flashing lights triggered a conditioned response and drivers did what they thought they were supposed to do. We were constantly waving them on to get moving and end the confusion, but the slow moving peace and quiet was a fitting tribute to a man who freely gave of himself in the interest of the community.

You go home feeling real good about runs like that.

 **RIDE 25 - 26**

The next day the Portland fall weather kicked in full force. It poured all night as I tossed and turned in bed, coughing frequently from a chest cold I couldn't shake. Before dawn I threw on every piece of so-called rain gear I had.

This day would be unique for the mere fact that I nearly killed somebody ten minutes after I walked out the door. The streets were soaked and the weathermen would call the rainfall 'showers'. My bike not giving me any starting trouble for a change, I turned on to one of the busiest roads in Portland, Burnside, running from one end of town to the other. A few blocks up the street from my apartment I reached the 35 mile an hour speed limit and saw three teenagers literally standing in my lane, the right hand lane, looking up the hill at the traffic coming from the other way. I pulled in the clutch and coasted, hammering the throttle back in sharp, loud jabs from the engine, going "Vroom! Vroom!" I always find that's a much better way to get attention than a Mickey Mouse motorcycle horn that goes "beep beep" like a sheepish goat. It sure got the attention of two of them, whose eyes were now solely focused on me approaching, but the other girl was still oblivious and looking up the street. I whipped the throttle hard a few more times but she still didn't clue in. She was seriously anticipating the opening between the cars in the oncoming traffic so she could cross the street to her high school, at a part of the road that wasn't even a crosswalk.

There was no where I could go, the left lane had a car waiting to turn left that made swerving not even an option. I was putting on both front and rear brakes as the space between us came at frightening speed, having got it under 30 miles an hour. I could see her ready to spring the instant a truck passed. Like many people say about accidents, time changed and everything could be seen in microseconds. I could envision the ugliest of events unfolding without me being able to do anything about it, smashing into her unpro-tected body and knocking her clean out of shoes and out of this world. I hit that throttle one last time as I came within ten feet of her, and then, my fears confirmed, she sprang into the street in front of me like a deer on a dark road. She must have heard my engine roar somewhat late, her head whipped around to see me and she screamed with every fiber in her being, shrieked in true terror, in a pitch so high, I can't even imitate, leaping out of the street, but not necessarily out of my way. I swerved to the left side of the lane and hydroplaned sideways on the sopping wet road for about twenty feet or so. Did I mention sideways? I think I did. At this point I knew I hadn't killed or hit her, but saw myself cashing in my chips on my first bad dump of a bike. It looked really ugly, unrecover-able, it was bad, then it suddenly snapped upright and allowed me to regain control. I couldn't believe it, I was so amazed and thankful I didn't know whether to go on or turn back and bitch that girl out. Lord knows, she had it coming. By taking her out she could have fucked up my life forever; years of therapy, nightmares, an attempted lawsuit by a greedy attorney her family finds in the yellow pages, a countersuit I would easily win but would be no happier for the legal victory.

I eventually did circle around the block and think I saw the girl walking under another girl's umbrella. Then I knew it was her when she laughed in a condescending way as she saw me. I told myself to forget about it. Just a kid being selfish and stupid and nearly paid for it with her life.

The first service was less than memorable, but the second service was at the notorious Black church that had been my first solo run. The service went way too long and they'd already called in complaints before I even got back to the office. One of the first people we saw when we got there was the gay hearse/limo driver who came up to us and said the deceased was a gang banger in a Bloods set. "He actually died of natural causes, if you can believe that," he said. Sickle Cell Anemia took him down at the age of 26. He called himself Peek, which is what everybody knew him as. He was one of ten sons. At 26, he was a father of two.

There were lots of guys walking around the streets and often into the service, wearing the baggiest clothes money could buy. We were all keenly aware that many of the gang members coming and going to the service on foot, many probably had guns and we wouldn't know it until they were in use. There was a three hundred pound dude hanging out at the door in an oversized red T-shirt, watching the street with as keen an eye as he could. You could feel the tension in the air, and we four white civilian police escorts with badges, not a single gun between us, as if it would make a difference. We were pariahs.

PORTLAND POLICE's Gang Enforcement Team had three officers there videotaping and photographing every person walking in or out that was under 30 and over 10. Later I overheard one officer wondering how to rewind her tape and she couldn't understand why her video camera kept shutting off. A well dressed Black guy, whom I believe was another officer, was perplexed as well. Knowing I could solve their problem, I approached and asked them if they were having trouble. It took two seconds for me to find the rewind button they were looking for to rewind the tape. Then she had me look at her video camera, which was instantly clear to me that the battery was dead, but not so much that it wouldn't come on for a second and blink before going out.

THEN JAWBONE CAME ROCKING UP. If there was ever a guy who was gonna cut corners and drop the ball on a run, it was this guy and his riders. This run was turning into a full on three ring show; gangs, police and Jawbone. He seemed to be a lot more approachable than the last time I'd seen him. We talked for a while and I found out that this church was not his absolutely worst client, but definitely in the top five. So, here he was, handing off his headache client for us to deal with. At one point, I asked him about my girlfriend's ex-boyfriend, a real loser, who claimed he had worked for Jawbone. When he realized who I was talking about he said, "Hell no. He never worked for me, not one day, not ever." He was so emphatic about it that it was an end-all answer. When my girlfriend later asked her ex how many times he rode for Jawbone, he wouldn't give an answer. Jawbone had actually refused to hire him because he knew about his four motorcycle wrecks and time in jail, among other things. What I found amazing is what a loser this guy must have been if he were to brag about working for a notoriously slip shot company that wouldn't even try him out, much less hire him.

. . .

Just like the last time I was at this church, the eulogy was a show to behold as it kicked into full gear. They were really making some noise in there and I went inside to check out the scene. The church was packed and the room immediately outside was standing room only. Hump stood out like a sore thumb, white guy wearing a yellow raincoat, helmet and a badge in a crowd of Black attendees. There was something more authoritative about him than me; his posture, body language, something I couldn't put my finger on. Maybe it was because he wanted to be perceived that way. He exuded it. I was far more more casual and everyone sensed that I think. I was able to see the minister at the altar through a small window in the door. He had those people in the palm of his hand, largely because that's where they wanted to be.

The minister tried to make his eulogy as passionate as James Brown in the Blues Brothers. I wanted to bust out laughing when he had the audience cheering his every line, some classic call and response.

He yelled, "We don't need no cocaine!"

The crowd would respond accordingly and he would follow with, "We don't need no crack!"

"YEAH!" The crowd yells.

"We don't need no gangs!"

A pause and then, "Yeah."

"Cause all we need is God!"

At one point he yelled, "It's God who gave the dog the bow-wow."

The entire audience would yell out, "Yeah!" or "Uh-huh!" or "Hallelujah!"

"He gave the cat the meow."

"YEAH!" "Right on!"

"He gave the cow the moo!"

"Oh yeah!"

"And the rooster the cockadoodle-do!"

One kid left the fine arms of his fine mother to stand next to me as I listened to the minister dole out the sermon. The kid looked up at me with big wide eyes for a while and quietly asked, "Are you a cop?"

"Nope. But the two other guys outside are," I said, referring to the Portland Police. I could tell he didn't quite know what to make of that, but think he was the only one there who really wished I was a cop.

It seemed as if the scene would be over when the minister said 'That's it' and announced the viewing of the body. I think Lenin had fewer people view the body than this guy. We could have been there until the sun went down. I stood in the room outside the church with the orange funeral papers in hand. As people slowly filed out, a kid kept asking me for stickers while his mother stood idly by. He must have asked me a dozen times if I had stickers as his mother just stood there, as if to test this white cop's patience. When the kid first asked for a sticker, I handed him an orange paper reading 'funeral', which had no adhesive. He held the paper to his chest, let it go and it fell to his feet. Stickers that did not stick would not do. He kept asking me if I had any stickers like a cop carrying baseball cards.

In the meantime, it had turned into a full on downpour outside. I went back out to talk about what we were going to do, at this point knowing the procession was going to be huge. One of Jawbone's riders showed up briefly, then supposedly took off to catch another service. Jawbone said that he was going to be late at another service and took off a few minutes later. In other words, he left us three guys to do all the work and bear all the complaints and idiocy of one of his worst clients; a typical Jawbone move. The three of us loaded the funeral flowers into the back of a minivan, running from a steam bath of the church into the cold rain and back again. Pretty soon, I was soaking wet in sweat. The coach driver, one of our guys, told Hump and I that we needed to clear the packed crowd out of the aisle because the casket was coming out. We slowly ushered the people out of the way, quietly saying, "Excuse us, we need to clear the aisle, the casket's coming out."

When we reached the church doorway, Hump opened the right side. The Black minister harshly questioned him, "What are you doing?"

Hump said, "Opening the door. The casket's coming out."

The minister barked back at him, "I don't need no pig telling me what to do!"

Hump managed to hold his tongue, but it got him all fired up. It's a good thing the minister hadn't said that to me. Who knows what I might have said as a knee-jerk reaction, but in my most civil of moods I might have said, "I'm no more a pig than you are."

The procession got under way, and as expected, it was tough. Three guys to handle a hundred or so cars, *a hundred cars*, that is a whale of vehicles to try to keep together. And to make matters worse, this whale doesn't want you to escort it; it wants to fight you, to defy you, to make you look bad in the process of trying to help them.

Instead of a well-oiled machine that functioned from a care at getting things right, this was like a jalopy, wheezing its way along to the cemetery, seemingly against its will. With that many cars, so few riders and a procession that goes out of its way to create problems, there's no way all of them are getting there together as one inseparable unit. They're going to get disjointed along the way, and they did. With one rider in the lead and two others holding intersections, there aren't enough riders to hold all the traffic lights the procession was taking up. Lights turn red as cars approach the intersection and there's no one to tell them what to do, keep going or stop for it. Confusion and resentment ensues. As all the cars took the last turn into the cemetery, one Black lady thought she would provide me with her precious insight and criticism, "You know, we left some people back there."

"I know," I said. I wanted to point out that there was at least a mile long stretch of cars waiting to get through the last six intersections, but I let it go.

 **RIDE 27**

Some days feel like one step forward and two steps back. This was one of them. On the road during the procession, I screwed up an important intersection, things just weren't going right, but then again, same for the rider up ahead by holding a right turn he didn't have to. We were all making mistakes. Minor ones, but it wasn't us at our best. Then I misinterpreted what the other rider was waving his arm for as I passed by. I thought he wanted me to keep leading the procession and continue what I was doing, so I kept going for a ways until I realized he meant something else. He thought he was signaling me to go on up ahead, to take off and go solo up the back route of the hill and beat the hearse, which was taking the slow route, to set up the last turn into the cemetery, minutes before the hearse would get there. All this, from a wave. Being unfamiliar with this rider and that route, I didn't 'read the air' and do what he expected.

As if all that weren't bad enough, I got lost on the way back from the cemetery to the garage. Nothing drastic or dramatic, just didn't know the most efficient way to get back to the office or how to describe getting there other than pointing and thinking like a caveman 'That way. Over there.'

Not a real confidence builder that day; but that's the school of hard knocks. Some of the best learning you do is from the mistakes you make. I could only hope this was one of those occasions.

24

RIDE 28 - 30

I t was my first triple header. On the first run with Hump and Hollywood, Hump and I nailed a tough intersection flawlessly, then had a great ride through the winding Skyline hills on the second run and nailed that beast too. They went perfectly, like how all rides should go, but not very memorable because nothing stood out good or bad. The third run however, I will never forget.

Hollywood had to take off, so Hump and I met Husky out at the final service for the day, the kind of full blown highly cultural funeral I'd heard about, this one being Asian. It's interesting how America truly is a cultural melting pot, but our different cultures and ethnicities remain isolated and separated. We see each other in passing at the Korean restaurant, the Chinese grocery store, that nice couple who runs the business we sometimes go to, but we never really get under the surface or see behind the curtain. It's all kind of on a superficial level of politeness and courtesy. You may be curious, but want to be respectful and not too nosey, so unless you're invited in, to a wedding, a ceremony, or a funeral, it remains behind closed doors to you. Being a part of this funeral was being in a position few outsiders get to see and to me, it was fascinating. This is all long before I lived in Japan and could identify any Asian culture on sight, living in my American bubble. At the time, I didn't even know what culture this service was.

Everybody had their role and part to play. There were teenage kids dressed in ceremonial white gowns, keeping straight and somber faces. Young girls and women were the designated cryers, quietly shedding tears for the departed. A priest sang a song of mourning to the sound of a bell or chime, incense was burnt, the whole sorrowful event was recorded in broadcast quality video. The videographer had a powerful pro camera light he wasn't using, with a guy next to him holding an umbrella over the camera to keep away the pouring rain falling outside.

Since the last service ran so long, we arrived late, only one minute before the casket was being carried out the door. We barely had time to hand out the orange funeral papers to the people before they got in their cars. One thing was for sure, it was unlike anything I had ever seen. We were told that *everybody* was going to the cemetery and wherever else they wanted to go after that. They were down for the full count.

Even though the cemetery wasn't far from the chapel, we had to take the entire procession of 50 cars or more in the opposite direction to have the body go to the home where the deceased had lived, and so off we went...

Not so long later, the cars descended onto a sleepy street of a quiet neighborhood like a flock of birds, parking the hearse outside the man's house. Imagine 50 cars trying to cram into the same cul de sac or park right outside it; like arena parking but in a neighborhood. Nothing we could really do about it except watch and wait.

With a pressing sense of urgency, the head guy making the decisions for the event said he wanted to cut the procession down to only five cars so we could get to the cemetery by 3:30.

He didn't really have to say it, but I knew the spirit of the dead man and his family would be in a bad way if we didn't get his body in the ground by 4 o'clock.

We got back on the road, now only five cars in tow, and were screaming through the rain to get to the cemetery on time. There was a real sense of desperation to get the guy where he needed to be so his wayward soul wouldn't be lost on its way to its spiritual destination.

Holding a left turn on a fast oncoming two laner, Husky had stopped one car, but there was another one flying down the soaking wet street toward him in the other lane. Laser focused on that driver, he didn't bat an eye. When the driver eventually saw him, that car locked up its brakes and slid four car lengths on the slick pavement before coming to a stop. Husky stared at the driver as if to say 'Are you done with your shit?' and the procession went on without incident. The man got in the ground on time, the family relieved, and we had done our jobs well. Husky was a freakin' rock star. I don't think his heart rate elevated one beat per minute during the run than when he was sitting in the break room drinking coffee.

25

RIDE 31

H ad a single easy ride with Hump. Was so easy, it wasn't really memorable. But before the run, he helped me out at the garage, cutting a four inch circular magnet off the back of a small speaker. Then he ground off the jagged backside with a grinder. I taped the magnet to the bottom of a small clipboard and wrote down the route and turns in big letters on a small pad of paper, stuck it right there on the bike tank in front of me in plain sight. I saw Hump make his own version months before and thought it was a great idea. I knew it would be especially useful for me, who could never picture the route in my mind when they would tell me the course. Without it, I always felt like I was flying blind, because, I was.

In the garage, on the shelf of the wall of tools was a clear glass mason jar holding a few pennies and a nickel. Someone had scrawled on it, 'Escort rider pension fund'. On the outside of the cooler where the bodies were kept, an official metal street sign had been placed reading, 'Reserved for employee of the month.'

 **RIDE 33**

I t was an early crisp and cold Saturday morning ride. Jackknife, Hump and I were pulling one funeral service starting at the Korean Martyrs Catholic church, this one another full blown cultural affair. As the casket rolled from the church to the hearse, a Korean guy was snapping pictures, investing a lot of effort and consideration into every shot. Like at the last big Asian funeral, this guy was taking his job very seriously.

As with such ceremonies, the family and relatives were pretty choked up. Two boys in church robes followed the priest towards the hearse, one kid had learned his bereaved bit quite well, heaving his shoulders every time he would draw in his lip in a momentary pout of fake sobbing. It seemed a little heavy on the acting side and he was laying it on a bit thick. I've read that some mourners like this are hired for the event, even kids, with no connection to the deceased, and he struck me as a likely one, trying too hard.

Passing out the orange funeral papers at Asian services like this was an exercise in reading body language, because most of them didn't understand a word we were saying. If one of the

people at the service didn't translate, we would have been
screwed. Even when all the drivers get the papers, a majority
of them don't turn on their lights because they space it off. It
looked like everybody had come out and I went inside the
church to see. One of the main Asian guys overseeing the
service approached me ever so humbly and said something like,
"Thank you very much. Much appreciated," and extended a
white envelope toward me.

I wasn't sure what to do. I guessed it was a tip for services
before they were rendered. I'd never encountered this in my
thirtysome rides and felt awkward. For a split second I
wondered what the company's policy was about this kind of
stuff, but then figured that I'd cause some bigger problems if I
didn't take it. I graciously took the envelope and said, "Thank
you." I could see through the white paper that it was a green-
back exceeding an amount of $5. It was a twenty. An instant
sense of guilt swept over me. Before starting up my bike, I
asked Jackknife what was up with that. He said it was all part
of their share the wealth philosophy. Share the wealth? I
thought, the wealth in death? What's that? To clarify, he said
the distribution of wealth was the notion that you can't take it
with you, so give it away. -And that made sense.

The procession was outta sight. Not a drop of rain, no
wind, just cold. We had to take about three dozen cars over
four major highways, holding back traffic from merging into
the procession and interfering. The ride went flawlessly, and as
usual, the radios went to absolute shit by the end of the run
and were completely useless.

With a good ride done and all in a good mood, Jack said he
was going to take me to some great place to have coffee. Little
did I know he was talking about the trendiest part of town,
Northwest Portland, gorgeous people walking around in every
direction. Well, the freaks and the beautiful people. We parked
the bikes parallel to each other a few feet from the coffee place.

We sat outside at some park-sized picnic tables, not by accident I think. Every eye walking through that intersection, driving by, sitting inside coffee places looking out the window, were looking at us, trying to figure out what the deal was. Sure, Jack liked the coffee, but I think he liked the attention even more, basking in it like he was getting a tan.

 **RIDE 34 - 36**

I was scheduled for a single run with Hollywood, leading me to expect one flawless ride without any problems. When I got to the garage early as usual, Hollywood found me and said, "Get changed fast as you can. Hump overslept. You've got his rides, just cross off his name on the triptix." He was really rushing me. Now everything had changed and I had new rides, including with some guy I'd never dealt with. I grabbed a radio, threw it in the bike sidebox, put on my helmet and took off.

The other rider, whom we'll call Meatball, was already at the gas station and had filled his tank. One tank that is. The other, was bottomless. I had only seen him once and these would be our first rides together. Hump had told me a few things about him, and he was sure right about one of them: Meatball was so hideously obese that it was downright disrespectful and disgusting. As I would soon find out, he lacked any redeeming qualities whatsoever; intelligence, charm, a sense of humor, empathy, thoughtfulness, all of these seem to elude him and were probably seen as unnecessary and non-vital efforts in the course of human existence. If he had a nickname, it was news to me and I never heard it mentioned, so for here, we'll just call him Meatball.

As we were climbing up through the winding turns of Highway 26 on the way to the first service, cranking in fifth gear, I could hear Meatball's bike chugging extra hard, like a little car with an overworked engine, straining to pull the extra weight. We arrived at an Asian church I had been to before, Vietnamese I think. As a relatively new guy, it was actually kind of typical to not know what kind of service was going on inside, the background, ethnicity, culture, or religious group. In a way, it didn't matter because everybody got the same level of service from us, like movers, but of a different kind. We spent most of our time standing outside waiting and didn't go inside so often. We mostly saw people on their way out, due to the time when we arrived and would have contact with maybe one person, the funeral director. Typically, we would check out the situation, the building, how big or small it was, and try to find where would be the best place to hand out the orange funeral papers so the most people would get them. Lots of people might go out a side door to the parking lot or something like that. We had to know these things. Shortly after we parked the bikes, the most beautiful of Asian women, my dream woman, walked into the church. I swooned in silence and think my knees got weak. She was to die for and then when I went inside, I saw there were a dozen just like her.

The second service was for a Black soldier, whose ceremony would be held at Willamette National, Portland's foremost national military cemetery. I had heard about these kinds of funerals since the first days of training, before they even let us out on our first rides. The American flag draped over the coffin, going to Willamette National, meant we would come to attention and salute. The pallbearers that consisted of mostly military brass lead the coffin to the hearse. My obese escort partner called, "Atten-shun!" and we all stood at attention and saluted. Speaking strictly from my point of view, Meatball looked ridiculous, standing there with his hand to his head and his belly sticking out seemingly two feet in front of him.

It was pouring down rain and I couldn't write down the route on the wet paper with a ballpoint pen that didn't react well to water. As like most rides with Hollywood, it went trouble free. Holding the last turn into the cemetery, it was services like this that made me outright proud to be doing this kind of work and being appreciated for the part I could have in it.

To put things in perspective, in many of the jobs I'd had before, not only were you not appreciated, but rather even disdained, like being a flagger on road construction projects. Not only the public, but most of the crew you're flagging for resent you. Or how many times have I started on people's wrong side first day on the job because word got out I'd been to college, guys calling me "Hey, college boy…"

THE LAST SERVICE was for a woman who in her younger days was a knockout Spanish dancer. There was an old black and white picture of the woman in her flamenco getup with the caption, 'In Her Entertaining Days', and by 'Entertaining', they meant outright jawdropping. Imagine Salma Hayek in her 20's in the 1950's and you'd have the right idea. Judging by the other pictures of husband, kids and family, it looks like her beauty, talent and charm had lead to her live the fullest of lives.

Standing outside in the bad weather, when Meatball heard the funeral director say there was a hell of a catered spread inside from the rain, it was like somebody had flipped on a switch in him.

"Free food?!" he said, and he beat feet over there in his waddling gait. Minutes later, when someone was calling him over the radio to ask him something, he wouldn't even respond.

We knew all too well he was in there enjoying the catered food to his clogged arteries' content, an absolutely shameless glutton if I had ever seen one.

The ride was tough just because of the rain pouring down that would not let up, bad visibility, just had to be extra careful about everything you did. There was so much rainwater washing around in my boots that when I put my right foot up to cover the rear brake I could feel a wave of water roll from my toes to my heel like the tide washing onto the beach.

28

RIDE 38

A single ride on Halloween. Another beautiful day, so gorgeous, I just wanted to get out into it. I was scheduled for a ride in the afternoon, so the night before I'd been playing pool and drinking with friends and now I had one of those rare, good hangovers, where your mind is on a completely different level and you don't feel all wiped out. I was loopy with a sense of appreciation of everything, like Scrooge waking up on Christmas morning. Ok, maybe not that much, but I was laughing at everything. Anything could amuse me. And everybody I came in contact with was laughing. They didn't know what to make of me. I was a different me, much better to be around, in rare form.

Husky and I had a lot of time to wait for the service to get out. We stood outside the church near the bikes for more than an hour. With nothing to do, it felt like forever. Pedestrians gawked at us insatiably, the passing traffic rubbernecked. At any given time I would look up and somebody would be staring right at us. People don't go to a funeral service expecting to see police I think, so it's understandable when people might wonder 'Hey, what's up with that? What are they here for?'

I noticed the hearse was so freshly washed the tires were still wet. Husky was reading the Oregonian newspaper out loud, an article about some of the stupidest things judges have ever heard in a courtroom. As he read each one, they got progressively funnier. People were still arriving at the service and I was crying laughing, trying not to be noticed. When he was done reading the article, without the constant barrage of humor, I nearly fell asleep on my feet waiting for that service to get out.

The doors of the church opened and people started coming out, walking not too far from the building onto the sidewalk. Pretty soon, everyone was milling around outside, waiting for the casket to be brought out, only about ten feet from where I was. Two women were standing shoulder to shoulder, watching everybody else come out when I overheard one say to the other, "Yes. Very attractive woman." Moments later I overheard another woman saying, "She must have taken over 200 tablets. I came home and did CPR on her."

Standing there waiting for the last of the crowd to come outside, I noticed something foul in the air. It took me a second to realize that not only one, but a number of these people were farting in conjunction, like a flatulence symphony. Had they all eaten the same thing the night before? I walked about fifteen feet away around the sidewalk corner, nearly around the block, but it didn't make any difference. And let me tell you, no single person could stink up an outdoor area like that alone. It was like a mass passing of communal gas at an agreed upon time and place, a coordinated gas attack. I had to wonder: What did all these people eat?

THAT NIGHT I went to the Monte Carlo, just down the street from where I lived, literally three blocks from my place. It was an old 70's style Italian bar and restaurant with spacious red semi-circle booths, like something out of a Scorsese movie, dark and cavernous in places. On Friday and Saturday nights, it was popular with locals for its karaoke, which was just taking off and all the rage. But tonight was Halloween and it was a filled to capacity bash I didn't want to miss because this year, I had the perfect look: Motorcycle cop. I strolled down there in the full getup, with everything except the helmet and a radio. I'd been there at least a half dozen times before, but not like this. The bouncer at the entrance, a total stranger, swung open the door like I was a VIP, didn't card me or anything. I think he assumed I was there on official police business.

The place was stuffed with people, shoulder to shoulder on the dance floor, music blasting and it looked like a throng you just wanted to get into. I was sober as a judge and wanted to get a drink first. Walked up to the bar and the young bartender guy seemed apprehensive, a little nervous about me, not wanting any trouble, like I'd come there to see if anybody was getting up to no good. I asked for a rum and coke, my typical go-to drink. He served it right up and I put the money on the counter.

Nearly shouting to be heard over the music, he said "Drink's on the house."

Now I am well aware that impersonating a cop is a serious offense and that is the last thing I want to do. I make it real clear to him, "I'm *not* a cop," and push the money forward.

He laughs and says "Yeah, right," and turns away to take another order.

I protest "No, seriously…" but it falls on deaf ears.

Apparently, my money was no good there. I take the drink and walk towards the pack of people gyrating in the middle of the floor, trying to figure out where to place myself in, or out of this situation. Standing room only.

Before I can really find a place to go, a relatively skinny girl is wiggling around right in front of me, arm's length away. She has her hands in the air and is shaking like she doesn't care, because she doesn't. She's wasted and that's all good and fine. It's the right mood to be in. She has her back to me then turns around and sees me, not liking what she sees. Clearly she perceives authority, someone who has come to rain on the parade. I'm in as good a mood as any, there to have fun and I'm sure my face showed that, but she felt that her female entitlement could show me that she could do anything she wanted, as rules and civility don't apply to her. With her arms still in the air, she raises one foot, like the Karate Kid crane kick, and tries to kick me in the balls. Not just playing around either, she's really going for it. She wants to see me doubled over on the floor in pain, like she should be allowed to get away with that and it's perfectly fine. -Because, obviously, she's a girl.

Naturally, my reaction to her is "What the fuck are you doing?"

Unfazed, she tries again, and again. I swat her foot away and bark "Knock it off!" And the girl eventually gives up because she lacks any semblance of balance. And that set the tone for how things were. I didn't know anybody there, and standing around by yourself makes for an awkward time, so I left, knowing the situation wasn't going to improve and probably just get worse. It was like running into that girl in the first five minutes was a bad omen.

As usual, I left that place in frustration and walked home not very long after getting there. Instead of the getup being seen as something fun, like the cop from the Village People or something, I was seen as a pariah, like the grim reaper at a New Year's bash. Somebody else would have known better and stayed home. Or somebody else could have rocked that uniform and been the life of the party. I didn't seem to be either one of those people.

29

RIDE 39 - 40

Husky and I arrived at the chapel and directed the cars where to park in the lot, which was a new experience for me, -traffic direction in a parking lot. Half an hour of that and we straggled over to a cafe within sight of the chapel. We sat at the counter and had some coffee, looking over newspaper pages, taking in the latest glaring headlines.

As we waited for the lengthy service to get out, there was a guy sitting two stools down to the left of me. Just by the way he looked I knew he wasn't playing with a full deck, his body language was all weird, but he hadn't said a word the fifteen minutes I sat there with my coffee. We were about ready to leave and the guy left of me starts humming, then he breaks out singing to himself. He turns to me, suddenly fully focused with intent, waving his finger and saying something like, "The Lord Jesus Christ has a plan for you. It is ordained." Oh brother I thought, here we go… He turns away for a moment, then turns back, ready to follow up, like somebody getting ready for a sucker punch. It's the classic tell that a cheap shot is coming, they turn away to try and fake you out, as if they've lost interest when in fact they're just warming up. I was already off my stool and heading for the door by the time he opened his mouth again. Husky knew what was going on but ignored it, not being the focus of the fanatic's ire.

"I'm outta here," I said as I walked by Husky.

I left that loon sitting with his words still in his mouth and no one to dump them on. That time in the cafe was more eventful than anything that happened during the ride. Runs with Husky tend to be that way, totally by the book and problem free on the road.

THE SECOND SERVICE was at an African Methodist Episcopal church. Everything was calm and quiet in the residential poor neighborhood, with the exception of a relentlessly barking dog. The church being in a poverty-stricken part of town, people were pushing their things around in shopping carts. It was an understood practice, when you're done with it for the day, to leave the shopping cart outside and if it wasn't there in the morning, the guy with the big pickup who's employed by the grocery store had rounded them up like stray sheep. I saw a few people arrive somewhat late and nonchalantly. Huksy took off to get gas, so I mostly just sat on my bike looking around, otherwise motionless. One guy came out and approached me courteously, asking if I had a cigarette. He wasn't thrilled when I told him I didn't smoke. -Cigarettes. From outside, I could tell the service was really getting into full gear, there was a lot of shouting going on by the minister inside.

Husky got back in time to see that once the eulogy had finished, a sudden, grim shift afflicted the people attending. In the time we were supposed to be handing out the orange funeral papers, nobody was taking them, they were far too distraught to even think about the drive to the cemetery. After twenty minutes, Husky and I hadn't given away a single one. There were at least four limos on this run and that's a lot. In hindsight, it all made sense. These people knew they were going to be in no condition to drive. I went inside the chapel to see what was up, the viewing of the body had turned into a full blown wailing, terrible mourning affair, almost other-worldly. I'd never seen with my own eyes so many distraught people in one place at one time; forty minutes of heartbreak and sobbing. There was nothing fake or overly-dramatic about it, they were losing it. Wild yells and cries filled the air, echoing off the walls. It was horrible, hearing the out of control wails of women having to be ushered away before having a nervous breakdown in front of the coffin. It was unbearable at times, the procession of young girls and women coming out in a state of almost hysteria. They would step outside for a minute, get somewhat composed, buck up and go back inside only to lose complete control all over again, come out in a flood of tears.

Wisely, Husky stood by his bike much of the time. He knew better than to go sticking his nose around in the grief of a crowd. In a roundabout way, I asked an elderly Black man what had happened that was the cause of such extraordinary grief. He told me the deceased man had recently had a heart attack, survived, was taken to the hospital, only to find out he was in the final fatal stage of bone marrow cancer. He died shortly thereafter at the hospital. When I read his obituary at the entrance, I was surprised to find out he was seventy years old when he passed. Even I would think he had more time to share with his family. He appeared to have a lot of kids and grandchildren and the sudden shock of their loss was over-whelming.

SUDDENLY THE PALLBEARERS and the procession started coming out the front and I opened the back door of the hearse, standing at attention. The deceased was also military, a salute and the utmost display of respect was expected. Husky was rushing to get his helmet and stuff on, knowing he wasn't going to make it in time for the salute. As the coffin was lifted onto the rollers in the hearse, I saluted, which no one could see since I was dwarfed by some huge guy in front of me. All anyone could see was my elbow behind his ear. Maybe for the better. They probably would rather I not.

It was a high octane ride, sometimes doing well over double the speed limit in the jam to the front to hold the next intersection; maybe in part because of the good weather, dry roads, and a no-nonsense approach to this one. There was no joking to be had, no laughs to be shared, devoid of any mirth. Only respect and a focus to do the ride flawlessly, which we did. There was no doubt the guy in the last car was blown away at least once if not a few times. I would be holding an intersection, standing on the bike like a poised dog ready to run, see that last car coming in the mirror like a target and the instant he would pass by, kick it in gear and take off like a rocket, rushing by him at mach speed. The cars in the procession are doing 30 to 35 miles an hour and I come screaming by within a few feet at 70+. I'm just a blur followed by a unique sound of acceleration they'd probably never heard before, and hopefully, not since.

 # RIDE 41 - 43

Another triple header and the first one would be an armful. Five riders, count 'em, five, to do one procession. The first person I spoke to at the service was the funeral director, who told me this was the same Asian church where two of our riders had gone down years ago, as in crashed, and one of them was killed. I didn't know the details about it, but the unspoken feeling in the air about this ride was that we really had to be on our toes for this one, more so than usual.

Knowing today's procession would be a whole lot of cars, they didn't want to take any chances, with almost everybody in attendance going to the cemetery. The run needed so many riders that even Jawbone had been called in. There we stood outside the service, killing time, one of the few times I got to talk to Jawbone. I noticed he has a way of speaking through what looks like his gritted teeth, barely moving his lips. I had to wonder if his mouth had been wired shut, and if so, why? I asked him how he made out in Reno the past weekend and he said exactly what I expected.

"I lost my ass. I missed winning my keno ticket by one

number. If I'd got one more I would have bought a 54 inch t.v.."

My girlfriend Muffin tells me he says that all the time, his missed number or if he'd only got that one card he needed, same as his compulsive gambler best friend, 'Smokey'.

The run gets under way and I'm riding in tandem in front of the hearse with the long procession behind us. Jawbone is riding his badass cop Harley up ahead with Husky. The bike is a beauty, but looks strangely unofficial, a modified street bike with red lights, like wearing casual clothes to a formal affair. Unlike us though, Jawbone hits the siren sometimes and never uses a whistle; too much effort. At our outfit, it's verboten to hit the siren for any reason and to make sure it didn't happen, they took them off the cop bikes we civilians were assigned. When Husky and Jawbone reached the intersection ahead, Jawbone pealed off his siren and got everybody's attention real quick. He didn't give a rip it wasn't legal and I yelled, "Go get 'em, Jawbone!"

We delivered the hearse and over fifty cars to a small cemetery I'd been to once before. Muffin first brought me there so she could put flowers on the grave of a friend killed in car wreck. The five of us split up from there and my next two runs would be with Hump, who was suddenly going by the name Doc because of his affinity for animals and what he perceived to be his seemingly magical ability to get along with them. Apparently, we now lived in a nickname democracy where you were free to choose your own. Guess I didn't get the memo; but the name Doc stuck and it was like we'd been calling him that all along.

The second service was at St. Anthony's church in my hometown, Tigard, right next to St. Anthony's Catholic school. -The same school my parents threatened to send me to if I didn't straighten up in their minds back in my elementary student days. Seeing me as a bit of a 'wild child', back then, I was getting in trouble just for jumping out of the swings during recess. That's no joke. Nowadays, kids get suspended from elementary school for bringing weapons, drugs, porn on their cell phones, you name it, but me, in the hallowed halls of bad behavior, I got suspended for, yes, jumping out of swings. Mind you, I had never landed on or hurt anyone in my high flying leaps, but just the possibility of it was enough to send me home to contemplate my misdeeds, which is why my parents took me to St. Anthony's for a check out visit, to scare me shitless. Well, it worked. The boarding school church-like atmosphere was an ominous, cold and scary place, run by nuns. I assumed they stood at the head of bible classes, 18-inch long hardwood rulers in hand, waiting to rap the knuckles of any disbeliever at will. Fortunately, I stopped jumping out of swings and never had to go there.

Of all the towns I could have a clear sense of direction in, it would be Tigard. I may not know the names of all the back-roads, but I sure as hell knew where every one went, with a flood of memories on every street and corner that was my stomping ground for fifteen years as a kid.

Doc would be telling me as we were riding, "O.K., we're taking this hard left here."

"I know," I would say, almost as if I were insulted. Any other town and I'd be begging to know which way to go at the upcoming intersection. The hard left was right in front of my junior high school though. I was the furthest thing from lost.

It was a nice slow rolling ride of about twenty cars through a residential neighborhood lined with tall fir trees, manicured lawns of green grass, bark dust and rhododendrons in the front yards, the kind of landscaping I knew all too well. There were kids' toys that had been left where they were last used outside their middle class suburban homes, tricycles laying on their sides, plastic baseball bats and other colorful things. Seemed like every other car parked out front was a boxy Honda Civic.

The unmistakable scent of wood burning fires in the air reminded me that this was where I came from and what truly felt like home. The ride was three miles long and took only fifteen minutes, just a quarter hour of a day's work, but what I would give to do that run again and savor every detail from every angle in slow motion.

The procession delivered to the cemetery, we turned back on to Gaarde street and started off to the third run, continuing down memory lane. I yelled to Doc, "Hey, I paved this road!" A few seconds later we passed my girlfriend's new apartment I helped her move into and would spend the night there that particular evening for the first time. Memories and connections were all around me, floating in them like an Olympic-sized swimming pool.

The last service was out in the boonies of rural Oregon City, the end of the Oregon Trail. Turns out it was Doc's hometown, and like me, he would get all sentimental when he rode through *his* flood of memories. We had an hour of time to burn, so at his urging, we rode to Doc's place. Turns out he lived in a mobile home park with his girlfriend and son from a previous marriage. We parked the cop bikes outside, greeted by his happy dog Buddy. The way he played with his dog, I could see how he broke his finger like he had goofing around with him, and why he had given himself the nickname Dr. Doolittle, or Doc.

Don't think it was my first time inside a mobile home, but I would definitely remember this one: There were fist-sized holes in the walls around head level, each one signifying a different explosion of temper that caused Doc's fist to go slamming through them. He made no mention of them because they kind of spoke volumes for themselves. He also had a gentle cat named Face that acted like it was chronically stoned, as if it were in some permanent dream state. He asked if I was hungry and if chili would be o.k. Sure. We watched home

videos of him fishing for huge ten foot sturgeon in the
Columbia River, as if seeing someone cast a line and wait
made for mesmerizing entertainment. Reeling in one of those
monsters, now that's good viewing, but that was not on the
tape I saw. 'This week on the Fishing Channel: We watch Doc
wait for a bite for twenty minutes'.

The service, way out in the countryside, was almost too
easy, came off without a hitch. After the run, Doc said he was
going to show me the scenic route through the winding backroads to the highway. What a blast, screaming through those
hills, dips and curves, going way over the posted speed limit, it
was motorcycle heaven. It's those rare moments that make it all
worth it, you can't believe you got chosen for this job when so
many others got turned away and that you're getting paid for
this. Well, barely.

We took a turn in front of an oversized white house in the
middle of some vast expanse of farmland and Doc yelled,
"That was my grade school!"

It looked like something from Little House on the Prairie
and smacked of the pioneer days when settlers first arrived
here. By the looks of it, I had to wonder if it even had wooden
floors when it was built.

It was a rare occasion and I happened to have my camera
on me, a beat up Pentax K1000 I'd been using since high
school, loaded with 400 ASA film. I'd asked him if he was up
for a picture or two, which he was. At the top of a hill I saw a
bunch of huge cows near the fence at the road. I had to have
it. Cop bike in front of a pasture of staring cows, not one of
them mooing. Just staring. In a perfect world, I would have
been able to get a shot of one of the cows mooing at Doc on
the bike, but it was not to be. There was an awkward silence,
all the cows still staring at us blankly. It seemed like somebody
should be mooing, so I did.

"Moooooo!" Still, no response. And yet, despite his magical

powers of the animal kingdom, Dr. Doolittle couldn't get a sound out of them either.

Doc in the countryside near some cows

 **RIDE 44**

The ride was from St. Anthony's church to St. Anthony's cemetery, as easy as it gets. Hollywood told me he was going to be sending me out with Doc a lot more often, especially since after the end of the month, Husky wasn't going to be doing the escort rides any more. He had managed to survive fifteen years as a motorcycle cop and was probably wondering what he was doing risking his neck day in and day out for this stuff. I couldn't argue with that. No matter how much you may love the job or feel the need to answer the call, there comes a day when it's time to bring it to an end.

Husky at the top of Mt. Scott

 **RIDE 46 - 47**

The first run was with Hollywood and Husky. Even though I knew exactly what cemetery they were talking about, I had no clue how to get there from where we were starting. We were pretty much in my backyard from where I lived, but things can get confusing when you're moving, like when you're told to take a right on generic Tenth, and then there's 10th Street, followed by 10th Avenue, 10th Way and 10th Yellow Brick Road. As I was in the lead at that point in the run, I held the right for 10th Street and the hearse driver did as directed, possibly to humor me and not cause problems, as all Tenths lead to the highway we needed. Basically, it was another ride with two pros and me, trying not to screw things up.

WE HAD a lot of time to spare before the next run and went to a nice restaurant for some grub. The second we got off those bikes all eyes were on us. Everybody inside the restaurant at one point stopped what they were doing and looked up. They don't know if we're there to haul somebody off for something or what. We sit down at a small, super-cramped table; all three of us could barely move. The conversation is always lively and interesting when Hollywood's around, his sense of humor takes over any situation.

Occasionally we'd hear the radio squelch loudly and some dialogue afterwards. Doc called out for me, "5-7 to 5-2, you got your radio on?" Hollywood picked up the walkie-talkie, thought about a response and said into the mic, "Nah." We got updates on everything he and Jackknife were doing until they arrived at St. Mary's, a couple blocks down the street. Hollywood reached the bottom of his chocolate shake and held the walkie-talkie to the glass, sucking the last of it through the straw for all to hear while pressing send. I'll bet they could hear Husky and I laughing hysterically in the background and it would be a dead giveaway.

They spoke of anniversaries with their wives and I couldn't help but get in a few words about my current girlfriend. Hollywood asked, "So this girl Minnie, what's her real name?" Apparently in the Mighty Mouse universe, the only girlfriend I could possibly have would be Minnie Mouse, right?

"Muffin." I replied.

"No, I mean what's the name her parents gave her on her birth certificate?" he restated.

"I told you. It's Muffin. No, actually it's Muffin-Jo. M-U-F-F-I-N-J-O."

They could hardly believe I was telling the truth and not pulling their leg. So far that had been everybody's reaction, mine too. Who in the right mind would name their daughter Muffin? Normally, my response to that would be 'I don't know', but, now I knew.

People from the table next to us adjourned and one man made a point to say hello to us. -The kind of civility you receive when wearing a uniform in public that speaks volumes about you, like a firefighter. We got three separate checks. I basically bought myself a seven dollar hamburger when I had fourteen bucks to last me five days. We got the bikes over to St. Mary's and parked them at various spots around the intersection so we could take off from different places.

I realized then that St. Mary's was one of the neatest churches in town. Spanish tiles, archways, columns, you name it. It's also the church behind where my biological father, Dave, was currently living. I hadn't seen him in quite a while, so I strolled down the hill to look in the parking lot behind the Acropolis Tavern and Hotel. His white jeep was in the lot, which meant he was either in the bar having coffee or was upstairs in his room. I asked Hollywood if it would be alright if I went down super quick to see if he was inside and say hello. There was just enough time and when I opened the door to the bar, walking around, heads started turning. -Motorcycle cop comes barging in the place like a terminator looking for John Connor's mother. I was obviously looking for someone in particular and wasn't finding them. With Dave nowhere in sight, I waited for the bartender to notice me waiting at the counter while she punched lottery tickets. When she finally looked up, she saw me, the badge, me again, the badge, and her expression showed she had a lot of questions she wished she could ask but waited for me to say something.

"Do you know who Dave Koester is?" I asked.

The bartender gave it some thought but looked perplexed. "What does he look like?" she said, wanting to help.

"A lot like me." I took off my glasses. "But older."

I got some quarters and called Dave upstairs from a payphone. He said he had a minute before leaving for work and I invited him to come across the street and see what I had told him was such a blast of a job for me.

A few minutes later he walked around the corner and saw

what looked like five thug cops in black leather standing at the other end. I walked down and met him halfway, shook his hand. He had shaved his beard since I'd last seen him and my grey hair was the first thing that struck him about me. Although it had been coming on for years, I had turned fully gray by the age of 28 and that was now. We walked up to the guys and I introduced Dave for what he was, my biological father. Hollywood was the first and only one to pipe up with an observation about the similarity, "You got more grey hair than your dad." -Which was true. I think it was from all the stress over the last decade, and what Hollywood said about outpacing my biological dad was the only confirmation I would ever get.

Dave really liked the bikes and the fact that my boss was wearing a gun, cuffs and mace. You don't see that every day. The doors to the church opened from inside and we all jumped to attention, the casket would be coming out any second. I told Dave I'd be in touch and that it was good to see him. It was a nice, brief meeting, as it should be, before the conversation became strained as usual.

Once on the road, we were changing from one highway to another and it can be a mess. All those cars not in our procession passing by, trying to get somewhere in a hurry, changing lanes, going faster than we are, not really knowing what is going on depending on their position, it's tricky to stay on top of it all. The whole plan went out the window once we were in the thick of it and nobody could hear a thing over the radios. Again, as always, they were worthless. Don't know what he was saying, but Jackknife was really talking in tense tones, indecipherable with the wind and the engine noise in our ears. Never did find out what it was about and couldn't have been that important if he didn't bring it up later. My guess is that it was just something that was bugging him at the moment.

Jack had been on so few escort rides in the last few months that on a beautiful day like this, he couldn't help but howl like a dog, going "Awooo-woo-woo-woo-woo!" for the joy of being out on the open road on a well-tuned bike. It didn't last long though. Despite it being his Achilles heel, he couldn't resist playing into his imaginary police persona and nearly intentionally bumped a car he felt was crowding him in another lane.

RIDE 48

Veteran's Day '96. It was a single run with Jackknife on a beautiful Saturday afternoon. The autumn leaves were exploding with color and the cirrus clouds made wispy patterns in the sky. We had a lot of time to kill so we headed over to that trendy coffee place uptown. On the way, Jack did something I couldn't believe.

Earlier in the week, Hollywood called a meeting of all the escort riders, seven or eight in total. One of his biggest concerns was what he called 'Contempt of Cop', an authoritarian mental state that kicks into high gear when someone breaks the law right before your eyes, even when you're in plain view, in uniform, maybe on the bike, whatever. A prime example is when two of us are doing 70 miles an hour in the fast lane in tandem, and some joker who's tailgating us goes around us and screams by doing 80. Some guys have a harder time than others resisting the temptation to right a wrong. Jackknife has consistently been the worst offender in this category, time and time again risking his job (and that of others) because he can't stand to see people flaunting the law in his presence.

Recently a car peeled out from a Texaco station and Jack

felt obligated to chase him down and pull him over, mind you: With No Legal Authority To Do So and gave the kid a good ass chewing. Over the years, I understand that Jackknife has played cop more than all the other riders combined. Part of his mentality comes from an incident where he ran into a burning building to save a little kid trapped inside. The Portland Police gave him a medal of honor and he was hailed as a hero. It obviously went to his head. He told Hollywood that he wanted to wear it on his uniform and got a big No Way in response.

One time Hollywood got a call from the Portland Police about him. He had been spotted on the cop bike at an overpass above a busy highway holding a *glove* pointed at passing motorists so that it looked like a radar gun. (Yeah, tell me about it.)

Veteran's Day was no exception to Jackknife's cop/hero/crusader M.O.. In fact, it might have been in over-drive due to this particular holiday, who knows? We'd just come off a highway and were waiting at a six way intersection.

A few rows of cars behind us, an ambulance turned on its siren for only a second in what was clearly an effort to get traffic out of its way. The car ahead of it made some room and the siren abruptly ended, the ambulance waiting for the light to turn green like the rest of us. Problem solved. Jackknife saw an opportunity to be Everybody's Mr. Helpful and leapt at it. He hit the red pursuit lights, moved into the middle of the inter-section and got everybody's attention.

'Oooh shit' I thought. I could see my job flashing before my eyes and how an incident like this could cost me it in one fell swoop. Jackknife waved cars through the red light so that a silent ambulance, in no rush, without passenger, could get through the intersection pronto. I couldn't just sit there and do nothing, the ambulance was also still behind me. I didn't want to get involved because I knew what he was doing was 100% *not* legal, but if I didn't back up my partner's play, I might have a bigger problem (namely, him, later) and it would be obvious we didn't know what we were doing.

I hit my pursuits and jumped into the intersection behind him. The ambulance drove by, looking at us like 'What are you doing?' -Which is the same expression a Portland Police officer in his patrol car had, only a few yards away, as I saw him waiting to go, totally perplexed. I could hardly believe the cop didn't swing after us and demand to know what the hell that was all about. He could have written us big tickets for that little courtesy stunt.

A few blocks later we passed the hospital where the ambulance and its driver were parked. Jackknife could barely resist going back and chewing the guy out for not going through the intersection when directed. That's how full of himself he was. He was fuming. When we're in a procession, we have about the same authority as a flagger on a construction project, but when we're not, we're just decoration on a traffic Christmas tree. Jackknife couldn't bear that in mind. Hopefully he wouldn't drag us both down in what appeared to be the twilight of his escort days.

 **RIDE 49 - 50**

T here were obvious tensions between everybody and Jackknife. In our minds, maybe not his, it seemed as if he was walking on eggshells. Our patience for certain aspects of his behavior was growing short and there was a lot of back-biting going on, guys talking about other people in not the best of lights. Despite that, Doc and I pulled off two relatively smooth runs with him without incident.

One of the rarely-used escort riders, name unknown or intentionally not remembered, was driving the hearse on the second run and he really puts the pedal to the metal, a real leadfoot, which was just an expression of his arrogance and indifference to having a cohesive run where everybody was on the same page. The basic idea of an escorted procession is for everybody to get to the destination at the same time as one connected whole, not a fractured broken up mess due to one person going rogue and doing his own thing. But this guy had a 'catch me if you can ' attitude, followed by 'I'll go as slow as I please when I want' and they'll both be right because I'm Me; grand, special, flawless Me, which was an all-too common attitude of some funeral directors and hearse drivers.

Sometimes, he'd be right on my tailpipe and I'd have to shift to a higher gear and take off. A minute later and he'd be dragging so far behind, we'd have to hit the brakes and wait. One time of many when I was checking my mirrors, I saw the entire procession but not the hearse, like it had suddenly vanished or gone to 7-11. That was because the hearse was so on my ass, he was in my blind spot and my mirrors couldn't see it. At one point, as the lead bike, I was racing to get in front of the hearse and he drove through a red light just before I got to it. He could have gotten wailed and it would have been completely his fault and no doubt, he would plan on blaming us.

Hollywood was waiting for us when we got back to the garage. He asked, "So what happened out there?" Nothing, as far as we were concerned, with the exception of the hearse driver trying to run us off the road. The driver had the nerve to say that we were going too slow. That escort rider/hearse driver was a major asshole 99% of the time, like it was his default setting. It was becoming abundantly clear that about one third of the riders were trouble-free and caused no aggravation, while for the rest of them, there was no shortage of attitude.

RIDE 51

It was my first time dealing with this particular funeral director and his outfit. Doc had warned me about the guy when we were still at the garage. Said this guy 'DC', as everybody knew him, was a maniac behind the wheel. He would blow through red lights before a rider could get there and lock the situation down. That's a great way to get sideswiped and be completely at fault, yet apparently, for reasons unknown or just dumb luck, this had never happened to him and he was pushing his luck with each procession. Eventually, his number was going to come up; or for us, the riders, putting us in dangerous situations that didn't need to be that dangerous.

It's strange how some of these funeral directors have some crazy notion that they have some greater priority or standing when they're in a procession, that the general public should instinctively know that they're coming, freeze when you see them, like they all should have looked up that morning and read the skywriting: 'DC coming through today, be on the lookout!' It's hard to believe that dumbasses like him haven't learned these lessons the hard way yet.

The first thing I noticed when we pulled up to the funeral

home was that the only limo there had its lights on and wasn't running. I tried the door but it was locked. It was obvious a real genius was the most recent driver. No one came out to speak with us, talk about the route as usual, it was the opposite of a typical friendly greeting by the person or people running the show and who want to make sure everything comes off without a hitch. This guy DC clearly didn't care about any of that.

I handed out every single funeral paper and told them how we were going to start. Everything was set to go, all the cars were running and waiting, I had got everyone to turn on their lights. -One problem, the limo wouldn't start because the ding-dong who drove it there left the lights on when he was driving in daylight and locked the doors. Didn't take long for the battery to die. I was the first one he asked if I had jumper cables. What am I, AAA? Obviously, no. Everybody was wondering what the holdup was and it felt like all the Black people there wanted to figure a way to fix the blame on us two white boys for the delay. One family member was bitching, and rightly so, saying "We're payin' for this shit." When I tried to tell her that the battery died because some doorknob left the lights on, she walked straight away from me as if I didn't exist because that's not the narrative she wanted to entertain. The story she wanted, is that it was somehow our fault.

Somebody waiting in the procession actually had cables. I popped both hoods of the cars and got on the bike, into place. With the limo started, we were ready to go and got on the road. That crazy fucker DC, in a red minivan of no distinc-tion, looking like any other car on the street, would run through a red light at slow speed with the hearse and the procession *behind him*, like he had diplomatic ambassador flags attached to the front. For some reason, he always demanded to drive the lead car, despite the fact that it's illegal. I saw him break two or three red lights with my own eyes before one of us could get there to make sure some car going through their green light didn't wail him into next week. How he managed to get away with this by sheer luck, again and again, is anybody's guess.

You know when you see situations in life, where someone or some organization isn't interested in doing the right thing or things the right way, because they're more interested in blaming someone for the failure or the mess they create? That's what was going on here and he was long overdue for a swift karmic kick in the ass.

 **RIDE 53**

I t was a cold time of year, so cold that all the bikes were now outfitted with what we call Hippo Hands. These are thick black hand covers that go almost up to your elbows so that our hands don't get stiff and unresponsive in the high speed wind. That was for when winter had started to set in, but when it got really cold, as it was now, we had a huge black heavy apron draped across our torso to keep our knees and waist from freezing up.

I was scheduled for two runs with Jackknife that day, but I also had a rare appointment at an eye clinic so I could get some new glasses. Things were far less convenient in that regard back then and getting glasses was a bit of a pain in the ass. Before we even left the garage, I knew that I wouldn't make it to the clinic on time, and if I wasn't there within ten minutes of my appointment, that was my last chance to get glasses under the Oregon Health Plan, so I had to make it happen. Fortunately, on short notice, Hollywood filled in for me at the church at the first service.

I headed out of the garage on the Kawasaki in the full getup so I could go to the clinic, get my eye exam done, then go straight from there to the second service. At the ophthalmologist's office, all eyes were on me (pun intended). Pulling up in the lot on the cop bike and filling out the paperwork with my helmet still on, being in a rush, drew some distinct attention. Nothing like a badge and uniform to get you that extra mile service, honest opinions and people walking on eggshells around you. Even a few women snickered, in a good way. Seemed as if the place was teeming with young women, like Wonder Woman's secret island, and I walked in the front door as Steve Trevor. I wish it was like this all the time, or at least that it happened more often.

After doing all the standard tests, like "Which is better, this one, or this one? This one or this one?" the doctor wanted to dilate my eyes for a certain exam, but I took a pass on that. Even though one can still technically drive a car without much risk, I had another ride that day and didn't want anything affecting my vision on the bike. I went to the reception desk to get the glasses prescription and the bill. Being my first time there and not sure how the process worked, I said, "That's it?"

The secretary nodded to her friend next to her and said, "Oh, and I need you to take Jennifer here to jail with you."

I laughed and smiled, at a loss for what to say. That's me, always missing or fumbling opportunities like that when they're laid at my feet. Moments like that, you can roll the dice of trying to say something clever and it will either be a home run or the strike that loses the game. As much as I might have been tempted to be flirtatious, I did have a girlfriend and just let my expression do the talking.

As I was leaving, sitting on my bike, draping the apron over me and starting it up, a very fine white woman came out of the clinic and checked me out thoroughly with eager interest. The smile across her face widened. This is a woman who would have seen me in the lot getting on my own bike in my normal clothes and wouldn't have given me a passing glance. It's likely she would have perceived me as some poor guy who liked dressing in black and probably had a criminal record. But with the police-like circumstances I was in, a respectable job and an intriguing getup that was the stuff of fantasy role play, she looked to be undressing herself in her mind and picturing me with the leather still on. The upper-middle class woman who wouldn't have normally given me a second look stared at me until I pulled out of the lot well into the street. As in many situations like this, sadly, I would never get to see her again or capitalize on that chance meeting.

RIDE 54 - 55

Two rides with Jackknife and he was getting on me about every little thing that day. After pumping my gas at the station, on a very rare occasion, a drop or two fell on the tank. I immediately wipe them away but Jack makes a big deal out of it, going on about how it takes the shine out of the tank and what lengths one would have to go to in order to restore its luster. All valid points, but he needs to chill out.

The first run was for that notorious funeral director DC, famous for thinking red lights don't pertain to him, but this time he was driving cool and not blowing through unsecured intersections. Maybe something had reeled him in or someone got through to him to knock off his shit for a while. If so, it worked. Without him making any unnecessary problems, the ride went fine, as it should.

We were screaming out to the next service at 85 miles an hour, terrorizing the highway, changing position before cars in the fast lane could even get out of the way, then suddenly riding the tail of slower moving traffic. This was all Jack's doing, as I was in no rush and knew we could get to the service on time. Once off the highway and on normal streets again, a

North Plains city cop went by in a cruiser then came back around to stop and talk to us. He didn't hit his lights or anything, but got our attention and made it clear he needed us to stay put until we could talk face to face. It was kind of like getting pulled over in place. His first question was who we were with, our unmarked bikes not having any city, county or state insignias. I let Jack try to square it away with the officer, as he had the best chance of clearing up any confusion quickly, whereas my answers might have lead to more questions and us being late to the service. Satisfied with what he was told, the cop drove off and went back about his business and we to ours.

We had wrapped up the easy second ride and were looking to get back to the garage before the looming dark and heavy clouds let loose their torrent of rain. When you're riding in tandem through any stretch of road, your eyes are scanning for so many obstacles, escape routes, scenery and other distractions, that you don't always see the same things as who you're riding with. Sometimes we point out things the other guy missed. At the last intersection before the highway on-ramp, Jack pulled up next to a blue pickup and was shaking his finger at the driver, barking God knows what at the guy. Didn't hear a word of it, but here he was again, playing Citizen Cop, unwilling to let the slightest infraction go unpunished. Just like flaggers who waste their time flailing their arms to get people to slow down, Jack expends a lot of effort trying to get traffic to go slower, basically so he can maintain his sense of control and order. Lighten up and let it go I say. Not Jackknife.

I pulled up to his left in the turn lane, having no idea what was going on, just him yet again getting bent out of shape about something. He pushed his bike back behind the pickup and waited for the light to change.

"Mouse, pull back. Pull back." he kept saying.

At the base of a hill, pushing backwards uphill would have taken me all day and I was getting pissed.

The light went green and after going forward a little, the blue truck got off the road into an Arco gas station parking area. It was obvious the driver didn't want to be razzed any more, so he pulled over the first chance he got. Can't be dinged for a moving violation if you're not moving, right?

Jack says, "Follow me to the Texaco."

We go to the other gas station across the street and he goes straight for the pay phone. I know exactly what he's doing, calling 911, trying to be the citizen above and beyond the call of duty. I don't even get off my bike, I'm just riding around in slow circles between the potholes and puddles of the truck stop parking lot. People at the gas station are wondering what the hell I'm doing so I say, "I'm waiting for my partner to get off the phone."

I'm thoroughly fed up with his pattern of behavior and just want to get back to the garage before getting soaked, not to mention it's the day before Thanksgiving. It's around 3:30 and the traffic is about to go to hell in the mad rush before the holiday. Jack hangs up and tells me to follow him back to the Arco station. Reluctantly, I do. At this point I'm asking myself how far I'm going to let this go before I tell him that I'm heading back to the garage on my own. If I show up back at the office by myself, chances are that the first question from Hollywood will be, "Where's Jack?" If I told Hollywood the reason, Jack would have some serious explaining to do and he knows it.

We sit off the road near the Arco station for a couple minutes and a different North Plains cop rolls up, sees us and stops next to us. Jack talks to the guy for a while and the cop takes the highway on-ramp heading out of town. The truck has long since hit the highway.

Jack says, "Let's help him out."

"*HOW?!* " I demand, but get no answer.

You might be wondering why I didn't say something or get in Jack's face about it but I knew the state he was in. He wasn't going to listen to anything I said unless it was "Let's get him!" Or "Right behind ya!"

We get on the highway a minute after the cop but I can see his lights swirling a mile ahead of us in the fast lane, the situation in the distance just a blur on the horizon. It didn't seem like the truck was pulling over, the driver probably couldn't believe what was happening. In no time at all we're doing 85 miles per hour again, scaring the shit out of traffic, making them get out of our way or going around them in a flash like we're charging to the rescue. Or, at least, Jack probably thought so.

The truck relents and stops on the side of the highway with the cruiser right behind him. We pull up about 50 feet back and sit there for a minute or two, watching the traffic stop unfold.

"I'm gonna talk to him." Jack says, and walks off to stick his head in this whole mess he's created. I stay on the bike and wait impatiently. Wasn't long until I revved the throttle a couple times as if to say 'Let's go!', but Jack was too involved in his pursuit of justice, literally creating drama where there previously was none.

As it turned out, there were no warrants for the truck driver and he was being persecuted unnecessarily. I didn't witness the reason that brought all this about and Jack never explained what it was that he thought he saw, but how bad could it have been if I hadn't noticed it happening right in front of me at the time? But I sure as hell wouldn't have called 911 to report a driver committing a traffic infraction that resulted in no perceivable harm. Witnessing a hit and run or a clearly drunk driver, now those would be justified calling 911 for. This was not it. We had already been questioned that day by a North Plains policeman about whether we were cop impersonators, and here was Jack calling the emergency number for a non-emergency and using the appearance of his authority to bend the situation to his will. He did so based on his suspicion and the outside chance the guy would have warrants and Jack could show that he had done some good. This is classic Hero Complex behavior, narcissistic in its origin and projects blame unfairly on innocent people so the hero can come along and make things right again. Sounds great, to the perceived hero. For the person on the receiving end?

    -Doesn't go so well.

 **RIDE 56**

D eath of a monsignor, or somebody high up the Catholic food chain, held at that cool Franciscan church I like. The place is absolutely huge, meant to hold big events with big crowds and this was a big one. I went inside to see what kind of sendoff they'd have for someone who had climbed the religious corporate ladder, because this was something I would probably never see again.

For those drawn to religion for all it's pageantry and ritual, this was the circe de soleil, a three ring show with all the costume and regality of a Broadway musical. A white Anglo-Saxon affair, played to a packed house, virtually all caucasian crowd. It all seemed so detached, almost clinical, the complete opposite of a family funeral with a sense of loss. This felt more like a system, an organization, laying one of their own to rest.

First came the hat show, where the head priest would take off one pointy hat to reveal another underneath. I thought it was going to be like a Russian doll thing, where he would take off big hats to display ever-smaller ones, but that didn't happen. One was enough. Then he started singing something so awful in such a terrible voice, I almost laughed out loud.

Came *that* close. That would not have been good, one of the escort riders busting out a laugh everyone could hear from the balcony, echoing off the walls of the cathedral. Every head would turn with a look of 'Who is that guy?' and could bring about serious consequences for me and even the company, so I quickly made for the nearest exit and stepped outside before I found anything else amusing.

IN ANTICIPATION of the coffin being carried out, we had to be at the ready near the back of the hearse, so there I was, standing and waiting. Chuck, the overtly gay hearse driver, was standing to my left. He's a riot and every conversation in his presence is fun. We were shooting the shit about God knows what, waiting for the service to get out. The walkie talkies we had being pieces of junk for a variety of reasons, without ever knowing when or why, sometimes the unit will go into voice activated mode without warning, and everything I say goes out across town to other riders on the same channel. I can just imagine, they're some fifty miles away, doing their thing, riding around, waiting for a service to get out, when they hear my idle chatter talking to Chuck, "Ha ha, yeah, tell me about it. That's crazy." Stuff like that.

The walkie talkie on the belt of my leather coat at my waist happens to hang in a suggestive position, with the antenna pointing upwards at an angle like some kind of overly skinny boner. I had no idea I was on vox but Doc came walking up and pressed the send button on my set, which kills the vox. I saw Chuck abruptly lean over to see what Doc was doing then snap back to his straight posture. He nudged me and said, "My God, I was wondering what he was grabbing. I figured if he could do it, I could too."

. . .

MINUTES before the casket came out, two long lines of religious monarchy came out again in their flowing white robes and decorated attire. More of the formality and ritual; this would be the big finish. I'd heard that the man had a place dug out for him in the hills of the highest cemetery in the city, a special area reserved for the dignitaries of the regional Catholic Church. Apparently, the elevation of the grave was associated with status, the higher the better. I'd also heard of how conniving cemetery salespeople use the idea of being closer to God for selling space atop a hill at a premium; that prime real estate coming with a hefty price tag, but cemeteries are filled with unordained saints, who I'm sure that proximity to their deity is not really important.

RIDE 57 - 58

Both rides with Doc and once again, the first one in my hometown and the second one in his. A blustery, rainy day, the last day of November '96. On the way to the service, we were waiting to make a left turn into the Texaco across from the funeral home and I saw a purple and red Suzuki Samurai with a cute girl at the wheel. Sure enough, it was my now ex-girlfriend, Muffin. After a few months of being together, we had split up because I didn't see us having a long term future together and better to end it on good terms than ending it with animosity or bad feelings. I wished I could have got a hand free from the hippo hands, but I was holding in the clutch. She saw me too, as the cop bikes stood out from ordinary traffic. She raised a hand and waved, yet there was a sad half-heartedness to it. I felt a slight twinge of guilt for having broken up with her, but it didn't take long to be reminded of all the reasons I had.

A dark grey cat that lived across the street from the funeral home was sitting on the hood of an old black Ford truck, watching the world go by, looking like it could use a five-minute friend. I came within twenty feet and meowed at him a few times. He jumped off the car and cautiously approached me, meowing as if to ask if my offer to pet him was really on the level. With plenty of time on my hands, I pet him for quite a while. That poor, attention-starved cat was so happy, he rolled around in the wet road in absolute joy, hopping up and coming back for more every time I started back toward the funeral home. He followed me across the street and sat under a parked car. I started to worry that he might get caught in the confusion of all these cars starting up, but then again, I gave this cat credit. He'd probably seen a lot more of these processions here than I had, being my first. I would pick him up and hold him near my shoulder, purring all the while, and land him on the other side of the street near his house, only to have him beat me back across the street again.

Parting with the cat back in the parking lot, the run to the cemetery took us way out into the foggy countryside, where after a while you could only see about a hundred feet or so. This was in prime Christmas tree farm territory, short, stubby little conical firs in long perfect rows as far as the eye could see, one tree farm after another and it was serenely beautiful. I love a good ride in the fog, everything so surreal and dramatic, along a peaceful two lane road, nobody in a rush, like a snow day, a calm seemed to have settled over the land. We had to turn off the beaten track to a rural road that wound treacherously up a hill, narrow beyond belief, wet and slick, with mud and gravel here and there. You wouldn't give it a second thought in a car, but on a bike, ugh.

The destination was a pioneer cemetery established well before the turn of the century, probably the 1860s, with tombstones in the style of days long gone, bearing etchings like Woodmen of the World. The backwood residents here must see a funeral procession like this once every five or ten years would be my guess.

On the way to the second run we were doing 85 along the

same stretch of highway I got pulled over by a state cop a few days earlier, doing 55 on my own bike. It seems he didn't like my aggressive riding style in his rear view mirror, seeing my headlight changing lanes too much for his liking. For once in my life a cop let me go with a warning, which made sense because I was going the speed limit but simply changing lanes doesn't equate to reckless driving.

Doc waiting down the street

The second service was held at a small nondescript building, in what seemed like the middle of nowhere. Normally, we would be standing right outside the event, sometimes going inside, handing out the orange papers to those in attendance as they came out, but this one was different. We would stay by the bikes almost the entire time, seeing the people come out of the service from far off. We nearly needed binoculars to see them. There was a feeling in the air that there were clearly defined boundaries, that our place was down near the bikes and theirs was well away from that. Basically, they wanted us to keep our distance. It wasn't just a feeling. We were outsiders and they wanted it to stay that way.

Fortunately, there was nothing unusual or challenging about the ride. It went orderly and smooth, without any mishaps or problems. For the second time that day, we rolled up on a pioneer cemetery on the outskirts of nowhere, but I'd been to this one before and once again, *hundreds* of people were already waiting there. I mean, the turnout was unbelievable. Your brain told you that something just wasn't right. It seemed so strangely out of place, why so many people would be in attendance at this old and small burial ground. I asked Doc what the deal was and he just figured that they were there for an earlier service, but that didn't make sense. Pioneer cemeteries don't see that many burials for the simple fact that most of the pioneers had long since passed away and they sure as heck didn't have back to back funerals on the same day. -Not to mention that if they were there for an earlier service, they would be in the process of leaving, not waiting for us. There had to be something else going on.

Jackknife told me the reason there were hundreds of people waiting for the hearse to arrive was because they were all Followers Of Christ, a fringe Christian group that has some pretty frightening doctrines. They're not allowed to see doctors when they're sick, but adhere to faith healing, which is basically praying the bad away, rejecting science and medicine, resulting in a number of high profile child deaths that lead to jail time for a number of parents. And when any member of the Following dies, the whole congregation turns out.

 **RIDE 60**

E very day when you wake up, scheduled for rides, you have no idea what you're in for, as in, I wouldn't know until I was told face to face what the situation would be. Could be a cakewalk or the mother of all runs; so there's no way I could have known this would be the toughest one so far.

All last week the top story on the local and national news was about the crash of a military C-130 cargo plane off the coast of California. Ten service members were killed and only one man survived. Minutes before the crash, the captain warned the crew to get on their exposure suits, knowing they were going down. The crew's airbase was stationed in Portland and the region was dealing with a great sense of loss, like when a natural disaster strikes, the communal sense of injury.

This was the worst weather I had ever had to ride in, a horrible combination of heavy rain and strong wind, like a typhoon, which don't happen in Oregon, but this was the closest I'd come to one since starting to ride a motorcycle. There were sixty mile an hour wind blasts, enough to blow you clean off the road if the right one hit you. Just riding out to the garage on my lightweight bike in a downpour was treacherous, much like the morning where I'd nearly killed that girl who jumped in front of me on a soaking wet street.

Extra early at the garage as always, but this time in order to recover and dry out a bit from the trip there, before having to hit the road again. Hanging out in the break room, I was starting to read a book about how to find a new killer job when Hollywood walked in and said he nearly got blown off a bridge from the wind blasts on the way to the office. This does not put my mind at ease, knowing I'm at least thirty pounds lighter than him, when you consider his height and how heavy his gun and bullet proof vest are. Wind gusts are the absolute worst for me, when everybody else seems to be riding through them without a care in the world, I feel like a kite or a sail, catching the wind in full, barely able to keep from getting blown off my ride, no matter how heavy the bike is. I can say that being buffeted and battered around in the wind is one of the worst things I experience when riding a bike.

Hollywood, Jackknife and I were getting ready to set out. Jack asked where our other rider was, Meatball, and Hollywood left to find out. He came back to say that he woke him up by calling. Meatball obviously wasn't going to make it on time and I didn't get the reason why he messed up, but he wasn't missed one iota on my part. As far as I was concerned, he could sleep in and miss work every day.

VISIBILITY on the way out to the service was for shit. The rain just poured and then would outdo itself for a few minutes, like the clouds are up there saying "Oh, you think that was bad? Well, here's five minutes of even worse. Enjoy."

My prescription glasses were just another wet windshield without wipers. I had to push them down my nose so I could see with my naked eyes which were pools of stinging rain and highway rainwater backwash from the cars and semis I was following.

Arriving outside the building where the service was being held, I was instantly struck by just how large scale the event was, the biggest I'd ever seen. It looked like a scene from a movie where they're waiting for the verdict of a major national case to be read on the courthouse steps, but it was solemn and somber, the news already known. Military personnel, all kinds of law enforcement, cop cars and bikes of all different jurisdictions, the media, videographers, photographers, reporters, family members and the general public all huddled together under umbrellas, lining the street and surrounding sidewalks. There was even an ambulance parked outside the building for reasons unknown, just in case somebody had a heart attack I supposed. The familiar patter of heavy rain hitting fabric and plastic umbrellas filled the air, cars slooshing by slowly in the street, unknowing drivers wondering what the heck is going on.

We waited quietly while the service inside continued, no usual joking or laughing out of sight of onlookers, this was best behavior time, remaining at attention for however we might be needed. Seeing a face he recognized in the crowd, Hollywood stepped away to talk to someone he hadn't seen in a long time. He enjoyed talking to his old friend only to find out he had been diagnosed with untreatable, inoperable cancer and had less than two years to live. He came back to us looking ashen, the color lost from his face. On top of that flooring news, Hollywood first heard that one of the crash victims was also a well known former Portland Police Officer whom he had known very well. In the line of work that Hollywood had been in for years, with daily dealings in the funeral business, hearing countless stories of tragedy, heartache and loss, these two hit home and you could tell.

From the main doors of the building where the service was being held, a bit of a commotion drew everyone's attention. Through the opening doors came Marines and Air Force servicemen, gently guiding the gurney of the sole survivor of the crash through the double doors, making extra-careful to not bump or jostle the man in their care. We all knew his face, Technical Sergeant Robert Vogel, having seen it so many times on the news. He looked a great deal better than his first hospital bed interview, but not well enough to walk, as they rolled him to the ambulance, still so fragile in his recovery as to not go by normal car or even be in a wheelchair. Then the casket of the single service member everyone had gathered for was wheeled out.

There was nothing to be said, with heads bowed, silence is the greatest display of respect. We stood shoulder to shoulder at the back of the hearse as Hollywood called, "Ten-shun."

We stood straight as could be.

He called "Salute."

I did, held it, looking directly ahead.

Handing out the orange funeral papers wasn't even considered due to the fact they were water soluble and terrible in wet weather. They would just turn into soggy strips of paper leaking orange dye. We, that being me and GM, the only escort outfit in town besides Jawbone, were telling people to turn on their headlights and hazards. GM is a big, roly-poly guy who looks more like a volunteer fireman than anything else. He rides a customized blue Harley with red lights, but looks nothing like a cop bike in my eyes. He told me it makes a terrible backfire when it starts up, but we were fortunate that didn't happen.

The grand procession got under way like an army decamping and setting off. This was unlike any family-oriented procession, this man was now a public figure. Bikes and police from a variety of jurisdictions, media watching and rolling video, it was full on. During the ride, I passed by a Lake Oswego motorcycle cop that was holding some traffic when his bike blew a fuse and everything died instantly, lights, engine, all at once. I thought it rather ironic, the police bike of probably the most affluent suburb in Portland and the state, instantly rendered useless by a blown fifty cent part. It happens to the best of them, as I so vividly recalled on one particular run.

I was holding an intersection as the last car with its lights on went by, then put the bike in gear and started cautiously towards the front by cruising up the oncoming traffic lane in the winding curves before the highway. Turned out the wind wasn't so bad, just a gusting nuisance, but the rain belted down on us like a rider's crop on a racehorse's ass in the final stretch. Wet leaves collected between the lanes in strips and piles, which is where I was riding, making just controlling the bike a challenge. It's times like these that I'm reminded of just how little rubber is touching the sopping wet road and what precarious forces of physics keep us upright instead of sliding right off the pavement.

As always, the procession would get bunched up sometimes and suddenly come to a stop in places. I couldn't see clearly what was in front of me with the onslaught of the weather and at one point locked up the brakes to keep from rear-ending a minivan, did a bit of a sideways slide, but recovered. Not much later, I hit a narrow concrete lane divider and nearly wiped out into the oncoming traffic lane. Didn't see it until I'd hit it. It was around six inches high at top, with two forty five degree angles sloping down. I'd never seen one of these before, guess it's a Lake Oswego thing. Needless to say, I ended up in the oncoming lane and was damn thankful I had both hands on the handlebars. One handed would have been certain doom, snapping the front wheel from my grip and going down for sure. I would have been a speed bump for the first three oncoming cars and hopefully the fourth would have antilock brakes.

It was a hairy ride for sure and I remember parts of it distinctly. Riding in a windy downpour, the fall conditions, gravel and wet leaves in the street, hitting weird things in the road without going down, these were all in a day's work now. I was getting used to it. I remember when they hired me they said that because of my lack of experience, I wouldn't have to unlearn bad riding habits. -Which was true. I was learning *their* habits, of being in the worst conditions, expected to do things a certain way and get it right, how to handle things, and when things go unexpectedly, as they would, to figure it out. Now, after 60 rides, I knew I could do this.

 **RIDE 61 - 62**

Two rides with Meatball. What a prick. I try and try to get along with him and tolerate him as best I can, but there's no getting around that he's an arrogant, slovenly asshole with the brain and culture of a housefly.

He's constantly criticizing me, cutting me down, speaks to me in a disrespectful, derogatory way, more so than anyone else. He kisses Hollywood's ass whenever he sees him because they go way back and Meatball is aware that everyone else knows him for the pigheaded jerk that he usually is.

He says that my writing down of the procession route beforehand won't help me any as we're going over the map. What the hell does he know? He and Jackknife are the biggest critics of my writing the route and placing it on the gas tank in front of me. They think my name should be Rand Fucking McNally when it comes to visually foreseeing the route along roads I've never seen or traveled. They can kiss my ass.

Having rides with him was something I did my best to forget about and move on, not to remember, however, I do recall that when it came to handing out those orange funeral papers, Meatball seemed to think he was above that and absolutely wouldn't do it. He wouldn't even hold them when I tried to hand them to him so I could grab something else we needed. Saw him screw up during the second service, but I'm sure I could never convince him of it, being utterly infallible in his perfection.

Our rides finished for the day, we sat on our bikes for what was probably seconds but felt like a full minute while the fog at the top of the hill at Mt. Cavalry Cemetery was awe inspiring. The noon day sun was peeking over the fogbanks and casting heavenly shafts of lights through the tree limbs and tombstones. I so wished I had my camera, I would have begged the powers that be to stay five minutes and get a few shots, begged dearly, pleaded on my hands and knees, the images I saw were so rare and moving. The last time I saw something so profound, art before your eyes that merely needed capturing by clicking the shutter, was back in the 80's at the gothic cemetery near my art college in the Bay Area.

Hollywood went left at a signal and I had to split right with Meatball. Later, we were waiting at a red light before getting on the highway, I commented on how gorgeous the scene had been back there. He acted as if he didn't hear me, then finally shrugged his shoulders and said, "Nothing to see up there but tombstones."

Yeah, exactly.

I have little doubt Meatball would hold a view of an all you can eat Vegas buffet in higher regard than all the wonders and creations housed in The Getty and Smithsonian Museums.

THIS MIGHT BE a good time to mention that I have a colorful and artistic history with cemeteries and tombstones. Those two lines in the want ads of the Oregonian newspaper that revealed this job jumped out at me like they were destiny, almost as if it weren't by accident, and it wasn't just because of the part about motorcycles. I'd had an obsession with cemeteries and tombstones since 1987, when I went to an art college in Oakland for a year. I was maybe, what, 18 years old at the time? Maybe 17. I lived in the student dorms that year and five other art students and I would get super stoned at night, listen to The Doors, then make a sneaky midnight trip to a humongous cemetery not far from the school property. But like a true D&D adventure, where unexpected perils lay around every corner, just getting there was half the fun. We had to cross this huge chasm along a cliffside ledge where the earth had slid away from the steep banks, about four stories above the grocery store parking lot below. There was one point along this ledge, only inches of loose footing to be had as you held on to the ivy-covered chain link fence to make the jump across, where one wrong move, one bad hand hold or foot placement, would mean certain doom if someone didn't take the situation seriously.

One night we found out just how serious the consequences were when our guide and mentor slipped and went crashing into the pavement, breaking his arm and cracking his head open. On other, more successful nights, we would make it to the final stage, the pristinely manicured golf course we had to cross to reach the cemetery grounds, which wasn't difficult at night, but I nearly got arrested once trying to do it in daytime and literally had to run into the middle of a busy street and dart between passing traffic to make my escape from an overzealous groundskeeper.

Navigating those challenges in the dark made it all worthwhile once we got inside. To see the vast expanse of tombstones, in styles old and long since passed, as far as the eye could see, was overwhelming at first, stepping through a hole in a fence to a wide open dark and ominous vista. The mausoleums and crypts lined the hills and the distant tree lines obscured any evidence of being in a major city. It seemed like the center of a new world and nothing existed beyond its unseen borders, as if you'd stepped into a theme park, where all the tombstones were real and all their stories were true. And we had the place all to ourselves. Not another living soul in sight or person to be heard. The only sounds were of the far off weeping willow trees, rustling in the breeze that seemed like a voice in a conversation, the wind in the desert, speaking to you. We could only answer with our minds: We are respectful; we mean no harm. The occasional owl would call out, as if to say 'Do you hear that? There are strange creatures among us tonight. Who are you? Who gave you permission to be here? Do not disturb this resting silence.'

Quietly we would traipse through the graveyard; tripping around the gothic tombstones and spooking ourselves shitless, imaginations running wild, senses bristling in their sensitivity. Some tombstones had a polished marble sphere at the top and the way the moon reflected in it was like the all-seeing eye that followed you wherever you went. We were the opposite of gate crashing hooligans or tombstone tourists trashing about; instead, we had a reverence for the place. Jim Morrison would have approved.

After maybe the second time, I came back the next day with my camera and snapped off some black and whites, the first time I'd seen the tombstones in the light of day. A leaning stone cross at the base of a willow tree, vines hanging in front of a black iron door of a mausoleum, a small statue of a child whose weathered cheeks seemed to have a tear rolling down its face. They were strong, powerful images. To me, they were art and profound. And like a lot of art, the images didn't tell you what to think or what impression they should leave, it was up to the viewer to find meaning in them, to conjure reactions that raise questions. They struck me as thought-provoking and intriguing. They symbolized mortality and our tenuous grasp on it, the eternal questions we'll always have about it, the monuments we erect to those who have gone before us or for ourselves.

A few days later, I showed the prints in my photography class and they grabbed everyone's attention, especially for being a subject so different and arresting. The teacher asked me "Where did you take these?" as if I'd traveled to the far ends of the earth to find them. They couldn't believe such a treasure trove of images was just over the hill a quarter mile away.

This started a lifelong interest in the subject. I eventually wrote a few articles for the trade publication American Cemetery Magazine, got pictures published in a national photography magazine and some other paying publications, but I did it mostly just to prove my work was at that level. A bit frustrated with these dark and less than positive images, my dad once asked me "Why don't you take pictures of butterflies or dogs or something?" and the simple answer was: Because I didn't really care about those things. Well sure, I love dogs and butterflies, but other photographers could shoot those subjects with better gear and a passion for them that I didn't possess, yet there were cemeteries out there waiting for me to discover and portray them in a way that was uniquely mine.

IMAGE GALLERY

 **RIDE 63**

I t was one of those days where the three local TV news channels had the town in a panic about some terrible storm they knew was approaching, so they had all their news crews covering weather-related stories to hype up the 'Big Storm of the Year'. Supposedly a monster wind storm was gonna come into town and kick our asses. Gonna blow us all away in a state where tornados and hurricanes don't even happen. And mind you, this is 1996, decades before the idea of global warming being a household term and the cause of mega storms. Weather-wise, things were still relatively normal back then.

I'd never seen Hollywood so concerned for my safety especially, as well as Doc's, and I would soon understand why. He was prepping us about what the run would be like, what to do, and to watch out for the idiotic hearse and limo drivers. The drivers were family of the deceased and didn't know a damn about how these things work, or don't work for that matter. The hearse driver was a girl, sixteen at best. Bad weather and bad drivers do not mix.

First turn out of the church was a left on Chataqua. Should have been the easiest turn of the trip. I set up the bike in the perfect position at a forty five degree angle for what was obviously a left turn. I have no idea what was going through her head, but that teenage hearse driver girl turned right instead and lead the whole procession the wrong way on the *first turn*.

'Aw fuck. Are you serious?' I said to myself. I feared to think what the rest of the run might bring.

I confirmed over the walkie talkies that she took a wrong turn and we had to adjust the route on the spot. Doc was holding a lane for the people in the parking lot to pull out, and not surprisingly, they were also acting like they suffered the same affliction as the hearse driver, so disorganized it was dangerous, making an absolute mess of the procession. Pretty soon, I was holding three cross traffic cars at a four way intersection for the clowns in the parking lot to get their shit together. The hearse and limo drivers were rolling through stop signs and red lights a half mile ahead as if they had God's own driver's license. Any second now some cross traffic car was going to slam into them without even touching the brakes, just full speed T-bone them. Little did they know the risk they were taking or that the responsibility for any accidents they got into would be on them, not us.

Turns out that the cars pulling out of the lot weren't going to the cemetery and I had to take off to get to the front of this disaster in the making. Risky business when the street is soaking wet like it was and all bets were off with cross traffic having no idea we were coming through.

JUST BEFORE WE were about to go over the St. John's bridge, I was holding an intersection and the hearse *again* went off in some direction of her own. Jesus Christ, what the fuck is wrong with this kid? Her second wrong turn, despite all our efforts to guide her. Not that she had any preconceived notion of where she was going, you could see on her confused face she was just going straight ahead. -Like the cemetery would just 'magically' appear in front of her at some point. Ok, time out! Stop the game! Reset and regroup. I held up the rest of the procession just where they were, dead in the street, stopped. Doc chased after the hearse, waved her down and escorted her back around the block. We got her back in front of the procession and proceeded over the bridge without the accident they almost seemed like they wanted to cause. We now knew how Hollywood's warnings and concerns were well founded. I just couldn't figure out how he knew it would be this bad.

Next up would be a new kind of challenge, getting this directionally-perplexed caravan over a steep mountain pass in the midst of a flash flooding rainfall. At Germantown road, there was a Portland Police car at the base of the hill, rain-water gushing over the ditch in a torrent. Doc had asked if the road was open, because if the rest of it was like this, it would be worth it to go the long way around. He told us the road was open but don't think he envied our situation.

As the lead bike winding up the serpentine road, over the walkie talkies, I warned of industrial trucks coming down the hill, slowing them down with gestures, warned of line crews up on telephone poles and their huge vehicles planted in the road. We passed massive mudslides from the year before and I would say over the radio, "I remember working to clear that slide a year ago." I could see Doc in my mirrors checking out the devastation, new and old. Trees that had withstood the worst conditions for half a century had fallen in the last two days, their white fresh wood testified to the recent forces bringing about their demise. We were in prime mudslide territory and one could happen at any minute in this downpour.

Now there were two foot-wide logs perched along the curves as barricades to the mountainous cliffside edges that many a car and motorcycle had hurtled over in decades past. I felt like some airline captain pointing out the scenery for the passengers as I called out over the walkie talkies "And those logs to your right are new since last year."

Despite the incompetence and recklessness of the hearse and limo drivers, our quick thinking and skill managed to avoid disaster as we delivered the procession to the destination without a scratch. On the way back to the garage, Doc and I were struggling to avoid the lake-sized puddles over the St. John's bridge, carefully weaving between them, with Doc a few car lengths ahead. No tandem riding through this minefield, especially on a bridge. Wiping out on a bridge would be like a worst case scenario. He said he saw the gigantic puddle as he passed it, but like times before, I didn't see it until I was right next to it. The semi-truck in the lane to my right, with its over-sized tires, wailed that puddle at fifty some miles an hour and the water blasted up over me like a huge wave crashing against the rocks, sending whitewater in all directions. I barely had time to crouch down, but the windshield took most of the blast.

Doc caught it all in his mirrors. He said what he saw was incredible, would've won the top prize on America's Funniest Home Videos, a popular TV show at the time, but it was actually better than that. It was a shot right out of a movie. I suddenly disappeared in a wall of water and then burst through it like it was a sheet of plate glass, giving the splashing water a second smashing. I saw him wave his arm with a thumbs up. I could tell he was busting up and his bike was weaving. He told me later that the closest we came to having an accident that day was him nearly dumping his bike from laughing so hard. It was the high point and a great end to an otherwise very trying and dangerous day. And I remember that moment like it was yesterday.

43

RIDE 65

Jackknife and I had a single ride in Hillsboro, starting from a church I'd been to once before that I thought looked pretty cool. As we stood around by the bikes waiting for the service to finish up, I was taken again by the design of this modern and stylish new building, so I was curious to see the interior. Orange funeral papers in hand in anticipation of the people heading to their cars, I went inside to have a look. A few steps past the doors, I noticed an arrangement of pictures on display on a couple of easels and naturally gravitated to them to see what they would tell me. I notice that I tend to check out these picture collages more than other riders, if they look at them at all, and one might ask why. More callous people might say these people are complete strangers and they're dead, so who cares? Well, I do. For me, it's because they tell stories, windows to the past, rich in detail and subtlety, a Christmas morning from decades ago, a birthday party, different fashions and hairstyles, just one expression in a single image can speak volumes, what the person valued and held dear, what their character was like, their brightness and positivity, or sometimes the look in their eyes of how someone or something along the way had hurt them and they carried that pain, it's all there if you can notice it. Read between the lines, fill in the blanks, and you get a pretty good idea of who they were. Of course, a few dozen pictures just barely touches the surface of the meaning and significance of a person's life, but I'm always curious, always interested. And in the funeral, like a final birthday, we celebrate that person's existence, sending them off as their story is concluded.

The service underway was for a young woman, nearly the same age as me, who had been tragically taken too soon. From the collage of pictures it was easy to see she had always been a God-fearing, upstanding, happy girl. She found a man she loved and who clearly adored her. They had three beautiful children, who looked to cherish their parents in equal measure. Pictures of the mother and father in a pile of leaves outside the house. Wedding pictures, graduation pictures, the studio portraits of the parents and kids. Always happy and full of life, they seemed to savor every moment.

When I asked one of the funeral directors the cause of death that brought this woman down in the prime of her life at the tender age of thirty one, I couldn't believe what I heard. She died of lung cancer despite the fact she'd never smoked a single cigarette, even though she underwent surgery to remove a cancerous lung, the insidious disease was tenacious and unstoppable.

I listened to the eulogy intently from the edge of the lobby, hanging on every word. I believe it was her sister who said that the woman who passed had such a courageous sense of humor in the face of adversity that once before surgery, she had written instructions for the doctor on her underwear.

I walked out of there on the verge of tears.

Many people learn these reminders of the fragility of life,

that someone you thought would be there for a long time is suddenly gone, that bad things happen to good people, that nothing is permanent. Although I did not know that woman, I don't remember her name or her face, she was then and always will be one of my reminders.

44

RIDE 66 - 67

The first day's run is in Oregon City with Doc and Jack. At the garage when we were getting ready to get out of there, Doc sensed that Jack was in a bad mood. I just thought he wasn't being his usual exuberant self. No biggie. Don't ask don't tell I figure. On the way to the service along the interstate, we were riding in the fast lane at just over sixty, Jack up ahead of us solo, me and Doc in tandem behind him. It was still upwards of 5 miles an hour above the posted speed limit, back when 55 was the law of the land. Doc and I could tell there was a huge wall of traffic behind us, afraid to pass, knowing they'd be technically going too fast. Jack is clearly thinking 'You're damn right they shouldn't pass us', and if somebody came screaming by at 70 miles an hour, he would tear ass after them to at least get them to slow down or get their license plate. Doc, on the other hand, like me, wanted to get out of the fast lane to let people go around. He signaled me to change lanes and I promptly did so. We sped up beside Jack who chose to stay in the far left lane and he saw us, but didn't want to change lanes or say anything, knowing it would go unheard with all the wind noise. Instead of opening a gate to let a flood of traffic behind us through, we ended up creating a bigger one with Jack's stubbornness, the three of us side by side in two lanes. Looks like another day where Jack got up on the wrong side of the bed and felt like taking it out on the world.

And as if to add to the aggravation, the rain then dumped on us for about five minutes and our riding formation changed every few hundred yards. Tandem riding was out of the question. Once again, water collected in the grooves of the millions of tires that had molded the asphalt, we had to ride to watch out for ourselves like solo riders, choosing the best part of the lane from one moment to the next. Doc would sometimes slow down for some reason, then come screaming by me until he was way up ahead. He was kind of back to that 'Keep up with me if you can' mentality, knowing there was no predicting exactly what he was going to do.

The procession went fine, nice and slow; in fact, it was the easy part, compared to getting out there. Doc and I had another run later in the afternoon, so he took off to go do his thing and pass the hours until then how he felt like, while I headed back to the garage with Jack. On the ride back to the office, Jack pulled over to the first phone we came across so he could convey to Hollywood what he thought of Doc's latest sign of 'rebellion'. Seriously, get a load of this guy. So full of himself he can't even wait to get back to the office to vent what he perceived as insubordination, over something so incredibly petty as not riding slow in the fast lane behind him like it was a presidential procession. Jack seemed to think he could call Hollywood and order a scolding for Doc like a sergeant calling in an airstrike.

Later in the day, I caught up with Doc at the same church as The Hearse That Went Thataway from a few days before. - The one with the teenage driver girl who had a penchant for going the wrong way. I got there just as the service was getting out, saw the people crowding around the hearse, Doc handing out the orange papers, and there was Jawbone milling around like a bystander. I hadn't seem him in a month or so. I knew that recently war had been declared on him as a competitor and wondered how he was faring. I was writing down the mileage of the bike just after I got off it when I felt something blunt like a gun muzzle pressing against my lower back. I turned right around only to see Jawbone's devious grin.

"Jesus Christ, Jawbone. Scare the shit out of me why don't ya'?" I said.

"Hey, Steve," he replied, thinking he was being funny. More politely than I'd ever seen him, he told me the route and I wrote it down, without a word of judgement or chastisement from him. He understood I had little to no idea about where we were going and wanted to cover his own ass by clueing me in.

Doc had told me Jawbone called him the night before and asked if he wanted to do runs for Jawbone and Doc wasn't having any of it. Jawbone was bad news and going down. He didn't have enough people to cover the runs the funeral directors were throwing his way, having to pull them all off on his own. In fact, he told me he would have to leave this run when the last turn was secured so he could make it out to another run he would have to cover by himself.

He then asked me if I wanted to ride for him and I tried to let him down easy. This was the nicest he'd ever been to me, and despite all the terrible shit I had heard about him, I had no specific event with Jawbone that gave me any reason to hold him in a bad light. He asked me if I knew anybody who rode motorcycles and the answer was no with the exception of himself, another guy already in the biz, and the guys at O.F.S. I told him that because I didn't know anybody who rode motorcycles, I had to take a Portland Community College course years before I ever bought my first bike. I mean, if he was down to asking me to help him out, he must have really been desperate. For some reason, he made a point to put a green rubber band over one of my mirrors and said, "That's all the rubber you're getting today."

When I talked to my ex, Muffin, later that day, she brought me to the dreadful realization that Jawbone might take on her ex-ex, Jughead, as a rider of last resort. This is the same guy who a couple months ago, Jawbone swore he would never employ, ever. I heard a day later that Jawbone had in fact called Jughead and asked him if he was interested in riding, and was he ever. What a potential nightmare that would be. Riding in a procession with my ex-girlfriend's loser ex-boyfriend is something I wouldn't want to see on a Twilight Zone episode, much less experience. Fortunately, Jughead's license was suspended in Oregon and Washington, and would cost thousands of dollars in traffic fines to get reinstated.

ALL THAT NONSENSE now out of mind, it was time to hit the road, everybody in their cars and ready to roll. It was by no means an easy route, a long procession that ventured down a busy, congested street for miles, then onto an interstate, back into town up Mt. Scott. A little bit of everything, but man, it was literally flawless, even with Jawbone.

After the run, I told Doc "Hey, uh, I think when you get back to the garage, Hollywood's probably gonna wanna talk to you."

He had no idea what for and rightly so. It took him by surprise, like being sideswiped or blindsided. I'd be blown away too. And it made even less sense why he tried to call in his wrath just on Doc, when I was in total agreement with him when it happened.

Sure enough, back at the garage, in the absence of Jackknife, Hollywood, Doc and I spent a good hour going over in detail exactly what had transpired that would warrant Jack's tirade. By the time it was all out on the table, Hollywood was in complete agreement that Jack was taking these little things way too seriously for the circumstances. We had nothing resembling a chewing out from Hollywood as Jack had desired, but something more like a praising for our handling of the situation. Hollywood said that one of the worst things that could happen is if one of us got pulled over for a speeding ticket. Jack, clearly was not keeping that in mind.

 **RIDE 68**

I t was a single run on an ugly, stormy Saturday in Salem, Oregon, the sleepy state capital. We get on I-205, about three lanes wide here, in the fast lane doing under seventy miles an hour and cars are passing us in the other lanes. Granted, we're speeding, but not by much. We aren't the fastest people on the road by any stretch. That didn't seem to concern the county sheriff in his cruiser coming up behind us.

Jack says he saw him closing in on us, but I didn't know what was up until the lights were flashing and we were getting pulled over. I mean, when was the last time you saw something like that, a cop pulling over what looks like cops? My guess is… never.

I thought we were screwed. On the side of the highway, the officer got right out of the car and approached Jack, as if I hardly existed. I got off the bike and stepped in closer to hear where this was going down. I don't know what made the cop go straight for Jack, but he had a pre-set lecture in mind.

"People out here don't know you aren't cops, you look like cops, you guys act like cops. You have to maintain the perception and live up to that standard. You are *not* above the law."

Jack spoke to the officer like they were on the same level, respectfully, but with a subtle sense that Jack and the officer shared the same profession. I didn't say a word; just nodded that I understood.

Jack thanked the cop and the officer drove off. Part of me wanted to blurt out 'So speeding in the fast lane, maybe not a good idea?', but I held my tongue. Instead, I asked him why the cop zeroed in on him and acted like I wasn't even there. Jack nodded to the chevrons on his uniform that could only be seen through his yellow raincoat at close range. Three stripes indicating he was a so-called sergeant in a private sector business. -A rank that was a small matter of seniority in a tiny company.

He said, "Because he doesn't have these."

Oh my God. I let out a good laugh at the absurdity of it. Jack could get a million more of those empty stripes and be no closer to the seniority of that cop, and that is apparently exactly what Jack wished he were.

He said, "I've done over seven hundred escorts and that's the first time I've been pulled over."

"Well, that's great for you," I said, "but my average is one in seventy."

WE REACHED Salem without any rain or further incident. Found the church easily enough, but the parking lot was so crammed full of cars, even the spaces between the spaces had been filled with people being idiots. They were packed in there so tight it made you wonder how they managed to get out of their cars. -Probably rolled down the windows and climbed out. They obviously thought some magicians, that being us, would somehow do our magic and overcome the incompetence of what they'd done when it was time to hit the road.

The service was for a thirteen year old boy who was a

passenger in a crash and flew from the car. Just horrible. The service itself went on for over two hours. We stood near the open doors and people would go out to their cars to compose themselves, pull themselves together and come back. Everyone was dearly hugging the devastated teenage brother that had survived. He just kind of wandered around the service like a zombie, no tears that could be seen, not a word to anyone. He was in a daze, I don't think he was even really there but more back at the crash site, still trying to believe it really happened and there wasn't any going back.

When people are so distraught in the event of such a tragedy, it's difficult to get their attention coming out the door, asking if they're going to the cemetery or not. My voice was especially low that day and to raise it to be heard over the passing traffic outside and the din of conversation inside was to sound like I was barking orders in some authoritarian, commanding way. That was the last thing I wanted. Jack's higher voice was getting people's attention far better than mine, so I kept quiet and handed out the orange papers he referred to.

A steady rain set in and the sky grew dark as the service went on. By the time we were ready to hit the road, it was half an hour before the end of twilight and it was full on pouring. Jack held the two lanes of oncoming traffic so I could lead the hearse out to the right turn onto the road. He was set up perfectly between the two lanes of traffic moving past the church, his red pursuit lights on his bike flashing, but what looked to be a securely held intersection wasn't 100% yet. Many drivers were paying attention and had already stopped, but not all. One car that should have noticed what was going on just kept coming, and coming, completely unfazed, until it finally locked up its brakes at the last second and slid on the wet pavement past where Jack was standing on his bike, nearly an arm's length away. It was ugly; one of the closest calls I'd ever seen. When you hear unnatural sounds of such urgency, like all four tires of a car suddenly sliding on pavement at high speed, you almost mentally cringe at the sound of the violence that might follow, but this time it didn't come.

Other than that, the run went fine. By now, it was the dark of night and the weather never let up. Puddles and troughs of rain below, wind and rain in your face above. Rode the whole way back without my glasses on in the downpour, wearing an open-faced helmet, my God, the hell of it. Once things get dark and without my glasses, the world turns into an unfamiliar place like fumbling around in a room at night without a light on, then you add in the rain and moving, ugh, it was bad. This was not working. I was really pushing my luck. The rainwater kicked up by the big rigs and passing cars kept the visibility to a myopic low, there was always some water being thrown at you from one second to another. If you're in a car, all these things are like minor inconveniences in your safe shell of a four wheeled vehicle, but on a bike, it feels like being on a pirate ship in a storm, the weather and perilous conditions giving you a good thrashing.

Just before we reached our exit from the highway, the traffic was backed up along the offramp, not like people waiting in a traffic jam, something was wrong, more like an accident ahead that was holding everybody up, we just couldn't see what it was yet. We put on our hazards and skirted up along the left side, where the mess seemed to be up ahead, out of sight. We reach the front to find there was a stalled sportscar boxed in at the edge of the lane with nowhere to get out of the way, causing this whole fiasco. There's a single flare on the road and that's it, no hazards flashing on the car or anything, so all the traffic is bunched up here at the problem, with barely any warning or ability to go around it. Jack gets there ahead of me and sees a blonde girl sitting at the steering wheel, just sitting there, waiting for a white knight with a tow truck to save her and her boyfriend. No accident or broken glass, nobody shook up or needing medical attention, just one indifferent girl and the boyfriend who puts up with her.

Jack started waving traffic around the stalled car as the traffic light less than 50 yards ahead turns green, but hardly anybody can go anywhere. The whole thing is just a mess. We need to get that car over to the right side, where there's some space out of the way so traffic can get moving again. Where it's at now is no good and will be causing this clusterfuck until a truck hauls it away and that could take hours. No civilian could just jump out of their car with a flagger's stop and slow sign, fluorescent colored safety vest and have someone else push this car out of the way, or at least it was very unlikely and hadn't happened yet, but Jack and I could make short work of it with the bikes and the 'officiality' of our uniforms, so we got right to it.

The girl's boyfriend and I started pushing the car out of the way but it only goes straight ahead, not in the direction we all seemed to understand it needs to go. Before we started, I said to both of them something like "Let's get this thing over to the right lane, over there," gesturing to where we wanted to land it. It seemed like we were all on the same page, what appeared to be understanding, comprehension, acknowledgement, but one person didn't even seem to know there was a book, much less a page to be on.

The girl in the driver's seat didn't have a clue whatsoever and just sat there complacently as if the problem would solve itself, that the calvary was coming and until they did, she could just tune out and everyone should just go around her and the car she was in. I have to yell out to her, "Turn right! Right! Get it off the road." She's five feet away and acts as if she doesn't hear me. Seriously, she has the driver's side window fully rolled down and I'm at the back of the car, but her cotton candy brain must be filtering out this stranger's voice. I can only imagine she hears something like the unintelligible muffled sounds of the teacher from Charlie Brown going "Blah blah blah blah", but when her boyfriend says the *exact* same thing, like a dog whistle, *that* she understands.

"Turn right. Turn the wheel right! The steering wheel…" he says, and she thinks 'Oh, I know that voice. What? Which way? Maybe this one. No, the other one.'

She is literally the kind of person when you say 'Raise your right hand' you have to say 'No, your other right.'

We get the car across a lane or two, but the girl got off script again and starts going straight, before we got it to where we'd been planning on going. Clearly, she thinks her boyfriend and I are going to push the crippled car to the closest gas station, blocks away (presumably so she can wait for a tow in greater comfort than on the side of the road), despite the space we're aiming for being just one more lane over. I yell, "Right! Right! Get it off the road!" and once again it takes the trained recognition of her boyfriend's voice to be able to heed a suggestion to make all their lives better. It felt like getting her to participate in helping to solve her own problem was like moving a mountain, and the heavy sportscar was an apt metaphor for it. I mean seriously, I can think of few other times in my life where I've seen someone be that incredibly stupid with my own eyes. As I'm fond of saying, ignorance is a choice. It's a conscious determination not to be educated, to strive for intelligence or common sense, but is instead, a willful avoidance of those things.

And it's worth pointing out, dealing with that traffic fiasco and the ding dong at the wheel, we didn't have to do any of that. As civilians, we didn't even have to so much as hit the brakes or stop to see what was going on, but there's a natural inclination to want to help. Jack didn't say 'Let's see what's up', he didn't have to. We knew exactly what to do instinctively without having to say a word. He set up his bike to direct traffic around the problem and went right to the driver door to see what was going on. As the angry cop that snarled at us earlier in the day had said, we look like cops and have to maintain that public perception. I wonder if he would have been so eager to bark at us on the side of the road if he could have seen us hours later.

Having got the car out of harm's way, the traffic resumed to normal and people were able to get off the highway when the light turned green, as they should. The girl's boyfriend thanked us while the girl remained aloof and indifferent as I recall; we had to move on and let them wait for AAA to show up and take it from there.

WHEN I WAKE up in the morning on the days of motorcycle escorts, the time that I get up to the time I get back in the door is time I chalk up to the company. The crappy part about the way we all get paid, despite seniority, is $18 a ride, whether it takes ten minutes or five hours. After taxes, the take home pay for a single ride is around $16, peanuts for the skill and training required, not to mention preparing for a single service, delivering it to the cemetery and getting back to the garage to finish things up can take up your whole day. That morning I got up at 8:30 and arrived back home at the stroke of 7 p.m.. After it was all said and done, I had sixteen bucks to show for it. Nobody had to tell me I was crazy for doing this.

Talking to Hollywood a couple days later, I conveyed my reservations about riding in a long downpour in the dark. He was genuinely concerned, but I was obviously nonetheless obligated to go on an afternoon Salem service if that's what it came down to. And whether or not I was hoping to look for a real, full time job, I was committed and available six days a week. I asked for only Wednesdays off, a day that I could call the right people or possibly interview on, and unfortunately, the best I could get from Hollywood, because we were so short of riders, was that I would be the last rider to be called on a Wednesday if things were really tight. Escort riders were in short supply that winter and it was obvious I had made myself a vital part of the remaining team. I'd almost worked myself into a corner by making myself needed at a company that couldn't use me full time but enough to keep me from looking for a job where I could make ends meet.

 # RIDE 69

A single run with Jack and I was feeling woozy from a blazing fever that kept me awake all night, tossing and turning. It was so dark outside from the driving rain I could hardly believe it was morning. I looked out the window and saw my bike suffering in the torrential downpour. This was all I needed. I was sick as a dog, would be soaked by the time I got to the garage, my run would take up the majority of my day, and I would only have 16 bucks to show for it.

I was muttering and mumbling to myself the whole way out there, "I have got to be out of my fucking mind. This is insane." Even though I had my glasses and full face helmet on, my specs would fog up and I couldn't see a thing through them. At least it was daylight, barely. Despite having my rain gear on, when I got to the garage it felt like I was wearing a wet diaper. It's a gross feeling with little to no remedy. I asked if Hollywood was around, and he was not. I was so spaced out that I couldn't tell the people in the office what I wanted to talk to him about because I couldn't really articulate my thoughts and didn't want to blurt it out. They had Hollywood call me at the office and I told him I was seriously thinking about packing it in, as in giving my notice.

I explained to him that December wasn't exactly working out the way I was hoping it would. If things were up to the company, I would work for them whenever they needed me, yet never make enough to pay the rent. They'd get by just fine, but I couldn't make ends meet and was getting deeper and deeper in the hole. I got out of the construction flagging work because of the miserable conditions, the unsteady, no-brainer work, and now in the rain on a motorcycle, again and again, I was just as miserable, it was a million times more dangerous and I had peanuts to show for it. I told Hollywood I couldn't justify it much longer. So many times I had been told by other riders that I needed to have a side job, like a full time side job, to pay the bills, and this was just for the fun of it and to answer the call, but I didn't have that gig and didn't have the time to look for it either. It was just a perpetual cycle of going nowhere. If I was going to make up my mind to leave the company I said that I would give them a two weeks heads up. It pained me that things had reached this point. And I had just bought some kick ass motorcycle boots for $130 the day before.

He understood, somewhat reluctantly. I say somewhat because I was well aware that as an employee, I left a lot to be desired and there were certain aspects about myself I couldn't improve in a short period of time, like not having an on demand detailed map in my head of the tri-county area. It was unfortunate that I was having to stand up and insist on time to look for a full time job, because the days I had left for drawing unemployment were quickly running out.

The ride that day was almost like an afterthought, with all that I had on my mind at the time. Fortunately, it was smooth and a piece of cake, slowly rolling through the countryside to Lincoln Memorial with only a dozen cars or so. No attitude problems or weird things with traffic along the way, just peaceful and easy like a good ride should be. The last car turned into the cemetery and Jack said, "Alright, Mouse. Take the left side and take us home."

RIDE 10

Two weeks before Christmas '96 and my hellacious fever, seventy two hours of pure hell, finally broke. I may have been out of the woods but I was still very much not myself, having just re-acquired the ability to keep my balance and weed out the fever dreams from reality. I'd talked to Hollywood the day before, conveying the severity of my situation, asking that I be called upon as a rider of last resort, if they have no other choice. Having said that, it didn't come as a great surprise when I heard on the recording I had a run the next day.

Didn't sleep a second that night, which had become my new normal. Insomnia was now a part of life; not as a result of this job, but my brain just never shut off or whatever chemicals were supposed to arrive in my head to tell me to go to sleep didn't show up. It seemed like the only time I could get any real sleep was when I was utterly exhausted or from drinking, otherwise, laying in bed was spent wide awake and my brain trying to calculate the last digit of Pi. I had the alarm set for 8:30, but when I saw the first ray of light peeking through the window, I jumped out of bed for the shower, like when you start your mornings off by saying 'Ah, screw it'.

A little rain was coming down and even though I'd put the cover on my bike the night before, now it didn't want to start up. -Part of that damn Yamaha Virago's never-ending starting troubles that came with it. So I'm out there in the street, trying to fire it up again and again, and it's giving me nothing but attitude. I know the battery is fine and in good condition because it keeps trying and trying. It's got juice. It just can't get the motor to do anything. Naturally, I was swearing up a storm, but not just a word here and there; pretty soon I was making new combinations of profanity like Newton inventing new math to describe the motion of the planets. I was that pissed off. Again.

So I keep trying. The only thing the bike was doing now was backfiring, like an acoustic insult, but still not the slightest sound of the engine turning over. I think I mentioned early on in this story that this used Virago was an absolute piece of shit, the most infernal contraption I've ever owned. I had compression started this hunk of junk more times than I care to remember, in what seemed like half the time I rode it if memory serves, but it was usually with the help of a steep hill to get a good rolling start. I didn't have that luxury here on these narrow, nearly-flat neighborhood side streets. I pushed it down the middle of the narrow road and managed to get up a little speed, maybe one mile an hour, popped it into second gear, let out the clutch and… nothing. Just came to an abrupt stop, not even a sputter. I did this again and again. And then did it again. Then a few more times. Seriously, this is how some men become infertile, crushing their balls while straddling a bike they're pushing, trying to get the damn thing to start. Better known in medical circles as Bike Balls. I was going to push this bike halfway across Portland if I had to. What choice did I have? What had I done to piss off these chaos gods and what could I do to appease them, because I couldn't do this shit much longer. Somehow, after enough tries, I finally got it to sputter to life and run like normal, but not before exhausting my plethora of profanities. I had run out of ways to curse that bike and the state of my life.

With my fever and exertion, I was already soaked in sweat. Just another day spent in the joy of my impoverished existence. I arrived at the garage in rare form, still sick but not as delirious as the last three days and nights, mixed with a fury at my situation. Kickstand actually said hello to me, which might have been a first, only because I said 'Good Morning' to him to acknowledge his existence. Otherwise, I have doubt he would have said anything, but surprisingly he said, "Hey there, Steve."

"What's left of him," I muttered.

I got my stuff ready and went into the break room to read my book about the educated job search, trying to research my way out of my predicament. Doc and I got out of there slightly rushed but made it out to DC's notorious funeral home without anyone noticing we were five minutes late. If anybody would seize the chance to jump on us about something, it was DC. Not two steps off the bike and I have to blow my nose. Next thing I know, I'm dripping blood like a hemophiliac. I see drop after drop hit the pavement.

"Uh, Doc, I have a problem here," I say.

He sees me bleeding like it's going out of style.

"What'd you do?" he asks.

"Nothing unusual."

"Pinch your nose," he tells me.

Now, I know what works for me and what doesn't, and pinching my nose standing up isn't going to do anything. I laid down flat on my back near a big bush out of sight so I wouldn't be seen if somebody came outside. Laying on my back, looking at the clouds passing overhead with the blue skies beyond would have been a nice last view of the world I was leaving.

My fever had me thinking a little loopy. 'What a way to go. Of all places, in DC's yard.' I thought.

My bleeding situation stabilized without anyone knowing, avoiding any scene or hassle, so we got the procession under way and the cars on the road. Right out in front with his stock red minivan, DC was running red lights as usual, that fucker. It's like he had a death wish he wanted to lay at our feet. Maybe he wanted to cause an accident and then sue us somehow. Lots of guilty parties turn around and do that with flagging accidents where a driver kills the flagger, so many work stories I'd heard over the years... The last time I saw DC, he had the nerve to say "Somebody barked at me on the last one," meaning someone had told him to stop committing illegal acts during the procession and putting our lives at risk. He didn't like it when anyone, especially white people, pointed this out to him. I hope DC wasn't expecting an apology because he would never get one out of me. Talking to Hollywood on the phone later that day, I asked if I was the only one who honestly wished DC got what he deserved: getting wailed by a semi-truck that has no idea why some guy is running a red light in a normal car. Hollywood said, "You're about 90th in line."

The run actually went smoothly and there weren't any hangups or hairy moments. I secured the last turn before reaching Lone Fir Cemetery, only five blocks from my apartment, in the heart of my neighborhood. Weird things can happen when you're working in your own backyard.

Doc was positioned up ahead at the last turn into the grounds, then started heading back my way. Strangely enough, right behind him was an off-color hearse, not black or gray, but a greenish faded yellow, heading towards me with one of our orange funeral papers in its window. Far from looking like an official working business hearse, this one seemed more like a novelty car, like the white hearse in Ghostbusters, but it also looked familiar, like I'd seen it before. It had that 1960's to 70's style, like how you imagine cars from the 50's or earlier, all these funky bulbous shapes in the car body, with fins and tail-lights that looked like rocket flares. I squinted to see if the driver was someone I knew and sure enough, it was my former next door neighbor from years ago, literally the next door over, from the apartment building I was still living at. We had that weird moment when we saw each other at a slight distance, almost in slow motion, with the 'Is that who I think it is?' expressions on our faces. When we recognized each other, we busted up hysterically with that, ha ha 'I knew it!' feeling.

After talking for a minute or less, we had to get out of the street, blocking traffic in both directions, which was fine, there wasn't much to be said. He'd bought the hearse as his primary car just because he was a twisted fucker who enjoyed the shock value of his behavior. It was for reasons like this that I had little to no respect for him, and for some reason, the feeling was mutual. He was the ultimate symbol of the average Portland hipster. He literally had no skill or talent to speak of and he knew it. If he possessed talent, I never found out what it was in the years I had of living next to him. He couldn't really do anything, so to compensate, he would grow his facial hair super weird, or get some tattoo he couldn't wait to tell you about or get his tongue pierced, or, buy a hearse. He even had a python in a big glass aquarium that he would feed live mice to until it eventually bit him in a life threatening way and who knows what he did with it, but I can guess.

I imagined him as a country boy from the midwest who came out to Portland with the intention of re-inventing himself as someone with style and urban 'flair', a permanent hipster poser, a person constantly creating themselves with a new tattoo, piercing or odd hat, to help define his personality, which is what he did every time he went shopping for accessories. He could literally buy his persona off the shelf.

In my mind, you want to be like a real Christmas tree,

where the tree underneath the decorations silently steals the show with its regal natural beauty. It's the real deal, and all the artifice draped on it doesn't take away from its underlying presence. You can decorate a fake Christmas tree all you want and at the end of the day it's still a shitty fake Christmas tree with a bunch of junk on it. Point is, my former neighbor was a fake Christmas tree.

He then drove away, presumably to go buy more of his newfound personality on sale at a vintage clothing store and that was the last I ever saw of him. To this day I still can't remember why he was there or why he had one of our orange funeral papers in his window. Why was he coming at me from the opposite end of the street? He wasn't in our procession, so how did he…? Why did he have…? These are the questions I don't have answers to but don't haunt me at night.

Doc and I were riding parallel back to the garage taking a turn through a residential neighborhood when I saw a big fat squirrel skittering nearly under my wheel, darting toward me then out of sight under the bike.

"Oh shit!" I yelled.

I braked and swerved and barely kept from crushing the little critter, only to have him jump in front of Doc, an avid squirrel hunter. Fortunately, Doc missed him too and we could see him behind us, scampering off the road in confusion. We kept laughing about it all the way back to the garage. If I had run over that squirrel, it would have tormented me to my dying day.

In the wind down after the run, we talked about the ride and the decision I had made about the job, as in to move on. I had given my two week notice. Starting the first day of '97, I would be trying to get a full time job, approaching the employment market in a whole new way and I was excited to get started. On my own terms, I would leave behind the most fun job of my life so far, instead of parting ways due to unresolvable issues, like getting let go as a result of my short-comings.

The incident with Jackknife from a few rides ago, the one where he called Hollywood from a pay phone when in fact Jack was the one being out of line, still weighed heavily on Doc's mind. I'm sure Jack wanted to forget about it once he realized he was the one who was dead wrong, whereas Doc couldn't get it out of his head. He felt he could never trust Jack again, never knowing when some out of the blue, childish tantrum would hit the fan and broadside him like it had before.

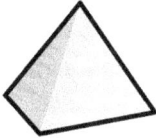 **RIDE 71**

I t was the last Friday the 13th of the year. There was good reason to be a little edgy on a superstitious day when riding with one of Jawbone's gang, which two other riders would be doing, but not me. Nothing scary or hairy for me that day, I had a simple run from St. Anthony's in Tigard to the cemetery a few miles away. It would have been given to me as a solo run, but the family had ordered two bikes and that's what they were expecting. That meant that either Doc or Hollywood would have to race across town to join me before the procession got under way, even though it looked like it would be a piece of cake.

I rode out to the church alone, which can be immensely fun because you don't have to think about tandem lane changes and the things you normally do when riding parallel with someone. Going out with another rider can sometimes feel like you're having to wear uncomfortable clothes, like somebody else's ill-fitting coat. And those rare occasions when you don't have to wear it can be liberating. It just depends on the person and the situation. Most of the time, it's great to share the ride with someone else and see and experience the same things.

At the church, waiting around for the service to get out, I saw two empty plastic water containers with handwritten signs on them, 'Pennies for the poor'. I guess everybody thought it was limited to pennies only because both jugs didn't have more than a dollar between them and only one had a nickel.

Like a number of runs during my time, I don't even remember this ride it was so easy. The chances of something memorable happening on such a short run, on a day with such perfect weather, they're enjoyable, not memorable. You remember the tough ones, the bad ones, the close calls, like bad students in a class, they stand out. You don't remember the well-behaved wallflowers.

After the ride back at the garage, I stuck around the office and break room for over two hours because people like the company owner, the secretary, Hollywood and a rarely seen rider I'll call The Pharaoh, had me dying laughing, whatever it was they were talking about. It was more entertaining than anything I could go home and watch on TV. If you could rig the break room for video capture, you'd have a broadcast quality sitcom right there, totally unscripted and spontaneous. And like this book, it wouldn't matter if you were into motorcycles, the funeral business, law enforcement, whatever. It's just about life in our current time frame, told through a certain context. It would be people shooting the shit about their latest attempt at doing The Atkins Diet, or asking "Hey, have you seen any of that new Fox news channel?" or telling about how everyone at the bar last night got up and danced when the Macarena came on the juke box.

And now that I think about it, what would you call that reality show?

"Coming up next on: Two Wheels and a Cemetery"

"The 90 minute season finale of: The Procession"

"This time on: The Escort Life"

Or to be totally predictable and unoriginal...

"Tonight on: Escort Bike Wars"

THE PHARAOH WAS a fellow rider I'd rarely seen around the office or rode with, but I knew he was also a cop. Weeks ago, he'd heard me grousing about trying to make a living with no full time work and not enough part time to make ends meet. He asked me if I was interested in making some money on the side and I said 'Of course'. Asked him what it was but he wouldn't say, that it would be better if he explained it to me at my place, he'd come over and tell me all the details. Sounded intriguing. I thought it might be security work of some kind, but for something unusual or specialized. Now the night of our meeting had arrived and he was knocking on my apartment door, standing there in kind of formalwear. My neighbor friend Paul had come over because he was as interested as I was in what this new income-generating opportunity was, the method of which could not be spoken of in the presence of others back at the office. Pharaoh put a DVD or VHS tape in the dual player (can't remember which it was) and it started showing some cheesy sales pitch and sure enough, it was Amway.

I was insulted. Who wouldn't be? I know he must approach virtually everyone he comes across about this, but it's hard not to feel like he took me for an idiot or a desperate mark for his pyramid scheme. Did he really think I was so stupid, desperate or gullible enough to fall for that? Maybe not, but hope is blind. Here I was in my apartment, insulted, a bit pissed off, and he was even being a jerk about it by saying I hadn't dressed up for his sales pitch in the same semi-formal way he had. What a jag off. But I couldn't tell him that. I still had to work with him and he was a cop. You never know when telling somebody off is going to come back on you, so I try to avoid it if I can.

As he was leaving, almost like a parting shot, he said:

"Normally, I would dress up in a suit and tie for such a presentation, but I knew that with Steve, I should dress for the environment."

-His actual words. My mouth was nearly agape by the time he finished the sentence and my friend Paul was equally amazed.

Things like that, it's hard to just blow them off and not take them personally. The questions running through my mind were: Does he think I'm the biggest rube he's seen come down the pike in a while? Why not break out three folded cards and we'll do some three card monte right there on the table? But most of all: How many other escort riders had he approached with his Amway gig and if not many others, why me? And even though I had those questions, I don't think I would have liked the answers.

 **RIDE 72 - 73**

F irst ride was with Doc in my hometown, Tigard, where once again, being in your old stomping ground can bring about unexpected chance meetings. At the service, of all the family that showed up, I noticed one particularly good-looking blonde girl. She did look a little familiar but I couldn't place her, didn't get a good enough look. Could have been anyone from anywhere in my many years of living there not so long ago.

Doc and I directed the cars on where to park, not like the drivers needed the help, but we'd been asked to do so. Standing around later, Doc proceeded to torture me with tall tales of his swinging single life, comparing my Friday night of staying home doing nothing, to his Friday of getting it on with some nympho blonde on a waterbed.

The service went on and on with lots of time to kill, but you had to be at the ready. You couldn't stand there and read something or stare blankly at your smart phone. You had to find creative ways to stand around without looking bored out of your skull, so I went inside the funeral home for the first time to look around. In the office talking to the funeral directors, I saw that Jackknife was our hearse driver. One thing was for sure, he was in this life and career up to his eyeballs. I walked down to the end of the hall and went into a dark room full of coffins, the showroom, like the floor of an auto dealer, all the shiny new models on display. I didn't want to turn on the lights, wasn't really my place to do so. I walked around silently between the caskets in the dark, taking note of how expensive they were. They ranged in price from $3,500 to over $7,000. I can only imagine what they might cost now.

As the service had just finished, people were coming out, mostly devastated, wiping tears from their eyes. I saw the blonde girl again and really recognized her this time. I asked an older woman if the girl's name was 'Chrissy' and sure enough it was. I never miss a face of someone I went to high school with. She was voted 'Most Athletic' and went on to become All-American at some sport. Back in high school, she did lots of sports, it seemed there wasn't a day where she wasn't excelling at one sport or another. At the time when people were coming up to me for funeral papers, I walked up to her and said, "Chrissy?"

She turned right to me like I'd flipped a switch, so yeah, it was her, but she didn't recognize me, which made sense. It's not like we'd ever been face to face or had a class together, so far as I could remember.

"Steve Edwards," I said.

She probably couldn't place my high school face at the time, but she knew my name, being in the same high school graduating class.

She asked what the heck I was doing there, as a cop at a funeral, like it's the last thing she would have guessed I'd be doing ten years after graduation. Steve Edwards, a cop? That just didn't make sense.

Our exchange lasted only about half a minute, then she had to go off somewhere and disappeared.

. . .

THE SECOND RUN was another one of those Followers of Christ burials. It was frightening how often they had them. That was the day when I learned the price of admission to their denomination. From the moment they're born, they're never allowed to see doctors, and as a result, the infant mortality rate is through the roof. Imagine if your close family and circle of friends and their families were never allowed to be anywhere near doctors or medicine, even for the simplest thing. Those maladies that could otherwise be easily treatable turn into something much worse, and soon are beyond control or any hope of recovery. Or imagine if one of them is in a car crash. No doctor. One of them has an appendicitis. No doctor. One of them gets pneumonia and all they need is some antibiotics to pull through, but no doctor, no medicine. You'd start going to a lot of funerals of those family members and friends. It would be like natural selection on steroids. But these guys, at the first sign of a medical problem, the prescription is more prayer. Strange thing is, I remember being struck at the time by the breathtaking beauty of some of the girls of the Following, the kind of nice girls you'd want to introduce to your parents. Standing around outside where the service was held, smiling, talking to one another, they seemed utterly angelic in their flowery bright dresses and nice clothes. They seemed like the fresh faced models you'd see in fall fashions of a Sears catalogue, all American looking girls. And it wasn't just once, but these two times I'd seen them. When I looked into The Following's current situation a bit online some 25 years later, I didn't see any of that.

THE PROCESSION WENT SMOOTHLY ENOUGH, as it usually did with that group. They never gave us any headaches. The cross traffic was another story. We were way out in the countryside, far away from any big city or the garage, I was in front of the hearse and it was my job to set up the last turn before the cemetery, but the cars gunning at me in the opposite lane were coming on one after the other, like no break in the cars to jump in. And they were screaming by at 55 miles an hour on this small country street, just within arm's reach. Everybody driving by seemed to think 'That policeman on the bike with its flashing lights can just wait his turn', but there was no light to turn green in my favor, no signal to fall back on. Seemed like we could all be stuck there for quite a while without a signal to break up this constant stream of traffic.

Finally, a timid minivan driver was able to see me and slow down, coming to a stop, but the driver behind her wasn't so understanding. What was this unexpected and unwanted interruption in the middle of this long stretch of road? She slammed on the brakes, tires screeching, and came to a hard stop behind the minivan; glaring at me for the disruption in her maniacal errands. Some seriously testy country drivers on this one.

Cruising up behind me as this was unfolding, Doc could see this troubled hold in the making, and distracted, fumbled for the grip on the brake and went off the road into the grass. I literally thought he might crash through a barbed wire fence until he managed to stop the bike before going into the adjacent farmland. But it was not good. Just lucky it wasn't worse. Something to laugh about later. The intersection now secured, the cars in the procession all made the left turn onto the sidestreet and after that, we were out of harm's way.

The rides back to the garage of such far away runs in the countryside were always nice. As with every time after having delivered the procession to the cemetery, the feat achieved, the challenge met, you no longer had to concern yourself with time or pressure. It would just be a quiet leisurely cruise through the backroads and highways until we got back to a major city. It was fun to go fast, but there was no rush, unless to escape the rain or traffic, and it was just kind of serene. Often these rides were almost without a single word spoken, it was just the sound of the engines and shifting through the gears, the wind in your face. You wanted to get back to the garage and for the job to be finished, but a part of you didn't want it to end.

RIDE 74

A single ride with Jack. I was in a foul mood once I learned that Doc had blown my Sunday night plans so he could get laid. He'd told me three days prior that Sunday was a big get together night of a few O.F.S. people. Friday, Saturday and Sunday came and went with no details of it happening or being cancelled. I was looking forward to it, would have been a first, but it was not to be. He later told me that it all fell apart on the day of so he could shag some girl he was chasing. No question, you can't blame a guy for getting some, but in the five or so hours when he knew the get together wasn't going to happen, he could have called and told me Sunday wasn't on. What also fried me is that it was so typical of my life, I'm left waiting around for something to happen with nothing better to do and I get blown off without a second thought so some guy can get some action.

Before the run, Jack and I got some coffee at his favorite 'look at me' place in Northwest Portland. After having been there a number of times, I knew that their standard coffee as they called it, was the utmost swill. Thick, bitter, with a horrible aftertaste, brewing dirt through a strainer would have been better. And yet, people were paying top dollar for it, having to do mental gymnastics to convince themselves it was the absolute best. I could imagine them saying to each other: "It's just so… earthy."

We arrive at the church right on time in a part of town I've never been to. We're taking the deceased to a military cemetery I was quite familiar with, so the route should have been easy to imagine. It was not. Despite knowing where we'll end up and looking at the map, I couldn't figure a simple way from the church to the grounds. Jack and our hearse driver go over the route in a matter of seconds, knowing exactly where they're talking about. I have not a clue of how to get on the interstate they're thinking of. Jack explains it to me, bogging down his description with so many unnecessary details it's impossible for me to follow, one after the other, "You know how we pass Hennessey, Geostum, Megee, then go under this little underpass near Holman's…?"

I've heard him do this before. He thinks everybody knows their local landmarks throughout town by their funeral homes, and that everybody in town knows these places. Sorry Jack, in my 70 or so runs, I haven't learned the spiderweb of funeral home locations all over town and every street that connects them.

I'm drawing a complete blank about what he's talking about because he has a habit of drowning his simple directions in a myriad of details that I've seen even tries the patience of Hollywood at the slightest variation from the point. It's confirmation I'm not alone in my thinking.

When I ask Jack again the directions to confirm I have it right, he loses his patience and said something like, "Aw, this is getting old. You've been on this route before."

Not true. You can go to the same cemetery a dozen times and not come from the same place. I wasn't about to stand around for any lecture or tirade he might be inclined to unleash. I turned and walked straight away, threw my cold shit coffee on the grass.

Jack feels the need to vent and is exploding on the only person around him, one of our hearse drivers, probably saying, "I can't believe how he still doesn't know these simple routes!"

I imagine the hearse driver quickly corrected Jack about a couple turns because right after that, Jack came up to me and said, "Sorry, I made a mistake about the intersection on 16th. We actually will be taking a left on there instead of going straight." -Just as he said we would in the first place, before he changed his mind.

The run went perfectly and smoothly, virtually without flaw. No radios, nothing. Jack felt that my job was in jeopardy at the start of the run, and sure enough, by the end of it all, he was telling Hollywood what a great job I had done. It was hard to take him seriously either way. His words of praise or condemnation were like noise in the wind.

 **RIDE 76**

Doc and I had a single run up to Mount Calvary that went really smooth, the weather good, the conditions ideal. As soon as it was done, he took off for another ride as I headed back to the garage on my own. This was very rare, at least for me, to ride back by myself. Even though I am not a cop and don't want to be one, there is a public perception while on the road and riding around. Until you get back in your civilian clothes on your own bike, you are not yourself and are in a certain 'state of being'. You might sit up a little straighter, not appear too casual, be all business, and basically, not look so 'civilian' and ride with purpose.

When I got back to the garage door at the office, it happened to be closed. I slowly wheeled up the inclined curb toward the security keypad when I slightly lost my balance, couldn't put my foot down because of a no parking sign in my way. The bike tipped over just ever so much and quickly went all the way over. Like ejecting out of a fighter jet when you no longer have control, I managed to get off the bike at the last fraction of a second before it took me down with it.

Man, thank God no one was around to see that. It took me

a couple minutes to get the bike back up and something just shy of a hernia. Sometimes I amaze myself; first of all for dumping it, then for the ability to singlehandedly get the bike upright again, considering the less than ideal position it was in. Sure, they've shown us how to pick up a bike on a flat surface with no obstacles, where even a small person with the right leverage can manage it, but this was different. It was on a sloping concrete ramp, so without the front brake held in, it wanted to roll away down the bank. I could have asked for the help of someone inside and got it right back up, but I wasn't about to go through the explanation and joking I'd get as a result. It was my dark little secret that I wanted to share and have a laugh about, but didn't dare bring it up. I was now keenly aware that nicknames could change, and it was still possible I could end up with a name like Dumper.

 **RIDE 78**

When you listen to the nightly message for rides scheduled to go out the next day, hearing that you'll be going out with some riders puts your mind at ease, knowing everything is going to go smoothly and there won't be any personality problems. Others fill you with dread of having to deal with them and their egos. I was on the roster to do a ride with Jackknife and at this point, it left me not knowing what to expect. It was a 50-50 chance things would go well with him on any given day, like flipping a coin.

It was six days before Christmas and I hadn't bought a thing yet. For reasons I could not fathom, I was feeling very positive and even…sunny. Could only chalk it up to some natural chemical mood swing. Arrived at the office two hours early again, where it had become so predictable, it wasn't early anymore, just normal. Jack and I hit the road when it was time to head out, everything went like it should. The service was typical, mostly just standing around, until we get the bikes and cars rolling in the street and the procession under way.

Early in the run, I was standing over the bike, holding an intersection in a quiet residential neighborhood, when I saw the red flashing lights of a cop bike and a hearse coming my way. This was unusual, seeing another procession approaching from another direction. Jack was closing up behind me and I pointed ahead, saying, "Procession."

"What?" He said, no surprise there. Was unusual for him too.

The cop bike in the distance looked just like ours, white with a big faring and windshield, definitely a Kawasaki, so it couldn't have been a Jawbone rider. The guy was tall and wearing all black leather, didn't look very civilian and sure enough, it was Hollywood. He reached the intersection I was at and said, "Hold 'em up a second." -Meaning my traffic, which I promptly did, stopping the cars in the street and having them stay there, like a train was coming through. He circled around behind me and waved the lead cars of his procession by, the first one being a red minivan with the notorious and unpredictable DC in it. Just like DC, who usually drives through red lights when we don't want him to, he decides to stop right there in front of me when he should be driving and says, "Why don't you let this lady go first?" -As in the lead car of my procession, which has already stopped and been told to wait.

It's an infuriating suggestion of such ignorance and incompetence, like when a timid driver waves you through an intersection when they have the clear right of way, and then makes a mess of things and causes an accident because everybody else is operating by the same understood rules of the road, in spite of the confusion created by the timid driver. It was worthy of me barking at him and saying, "Why don't you shut the fuck up and keep driving?" -But I didn't. I just ignored him because Hollywood was right there. Had he not been there, I probably would have offered up some choice words that surely would have had him calling the office to complain before the sun went down. Figuring DC out was pretty simple when it came to how he dealt with us, he seemed to think 'How can I mess things up for them and always try to make those white cops look bad?' And try and try he did, with little to no success.

Turns out that in Hollywood's run, before he met up with us in the street, DC was totally against the best way to get to the cemetery for the sake that he wanted to drive the hearse and all the rented limousines through the heart of the Black neighborhood for some good, free advertising at the expense of the bereaving family. Made him look good in the community, so he would milk it, taking the scenic route. For DC, it was like a parade.

Hollywood's ride was done once he got DC and that traffic off his hands, but Jack and I were just getting started. We had a long way to go. Hollywood rode off. Cruising down a certain street, maybe it was called Why Can't You Remember This Avenue, I should have stopped to secure a particular side street I'd missed before on a previous run. Not having a hold of a side street is like having a door open in a long hallway of doors when you want them all shut. Something could unexpectedly come out of one of those doors and bone everything. Such flaws almost always go unnoticed by the procession but are never missed by a senior rider. Why I'd missed that one twice was the question.

Going over the Fremont bridge and along Interstate 405, I'm coming up from the back between the cars and see Jack up ahead, riding alongside the hearse driver, trying to communicate something. Jack sees me coming in his mirrors and he's waving frantically for me to slow down; I have no idea why. I pull up beside him to see what the hell he wants and he yells, "Slow down!" Not two seconds go by and he's barking, "Get in front of the hearse!"

That's exactly what I was doing until he waved me in to bark at me to hurry up and slow down in executing my task. Rarely do I get pissed off and bitch in these rides, but I was yelling to myself, "Make up you freaking mind! Speed up, slow down, what the fuck?!"

Jack was watching a truck behind us that was wanting to merge with the procession and he was waving like a madman for the guy to speed up and go around us, but was obviously pleading with someone who didn't want to do that. I thought Jack was going to bust a vein before he'd get that guy to go around us, but eventually he did. I just rode along, shaking my head, thinking, 'Let it go, man. Take it easy. Don't have a heart attack.'

Just like before when he got bent out of shape about Doc and called Hollywood from a payphone, he wanted to bitch me out and assert his authority as soon as possible. The problem was that his way of speaking was overtly derogatory and I had no patience for it. At one intersection I was holding, he rode up next to me and thought he was going to launch into his second salvo, but I cut him off, "Jack, I don't have to take your tone of voice," and rode off to where I was needed next.

The last car having turned into the cemetery, we'd pulled off another somewhat smooth ride. I put the bike in gear and rode down to the cemetery entrance, the starting point for the ride back to the office, and waited. Less than a minute later, he rode down beside me, and like a child in a huff who didn't get to bitch me out as he'd wanted, he said, "See you back at the shop."

Fine by me. Riding back to the office solo is just the way I'd have it. I follow him down the hill to the first stop light and wait beside him, ignoring his uptight presence.

He immediately apologizes, saying something like, "I didn't mean to come off like I was barking at you," and I was tempted to say, "Well then you failed miserably", but I was in too good of a mood to make a scene.

That's the interesting thing in retrospect. If he had tried to bite my head off like he had that day when I was in a foul mood a few days before, he would have got it right back both barrels. I would have made verbal short time of him and had a huge fight on my hands. No doubt, he would take it to Hollywood just to bring me to heel and call in a scolding like he'd tried to do when he felt Doc was being spiteful. So I was biding my time to avoid that, seeing him as a pot that was about to boil over.

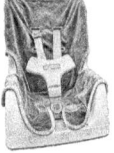 **RIDE 79 - 81**

It was a rainy morning and the clouds were unloading on us like exposed targets in a barrage. Rain gear, though useful, is often times useless. Better to have it than not, but you get soaking wet one way or another. Rainy times are inherently humid and the plastic rain gear traps all the heat and steam you're giving off, so you get wet from the inside out. The best way to look at rain gear is how long it can keep a full soaking at bay because you're just buying time.

During the first run, Hollywood told me to hold the back door of the procession, following the last car and not allowing any traffic to merge with our cars even though there were two lanes. As I tailgated the last car between the lanes, I saw a familiar truck in my mirror, then the driver waving, getting my attention. Sure enough, it was one of the construction workers I had worked with and carpooled with for years. Took me a second to really believe it, the fact that he recognized me *from behind* in the cop uniform, on a moving bike, was pretty amazing. He pulled up to my left, rolled down his passenger window and we yelled a brief conversation between us.

"Hey Dan! How ya' doin', man?!"

He was on his way to work on this dreary Saturday, stuck with that company as far as I was concerned. It gave me a boost to feel free and clear of that dead end job. Couldn't really say I was in a better situation, but I had been liberated and was not trapped in a go nowhere job.

By the end of that first run, Hollywood, Doc, Jack and I were like a bunch of wet cats that couldn't get out of the rain and were thoroughly miserable for it. On the second run, Hollywood wouldn't let me write down the streets and turns for my clipboard on my tank. He wanted me to either understand it beforehand, or memorize it and figure it out along the way, on roads I'd never traveled. When he was done explaining the route, he asked me to repeat it back to him when I knew full well I couldn't. I could only remember the first three roads of a dozen, and whether we went left or right was largely just a guess. I hate going on a run flying blind like that. I spend the whole time wanting to say, "Here?!"

The rain was really coming down, making my specs worthless. It got real dark for a while and suddenly I could hardly see my *speedometer*, much less the damn street signs. And here I was leading the procession ahead of Hollywood and Jack. I drove right by Shattuck Road, the one I was supposed to hold for a right turn. I thought it would be the green lights ahead but it was a little side street I didn't see whatsoever. What I did see was Hollywood and Jack turning right a quarter mile behind me. Even with 80 rides under my belt, Hollywood wouldn't send me out solo because he knew I'd be completely lost, no matter where you dropped me.

The third service was for a guy who'd passed away around the age of 62. While waiting at the service, I looked closely over the collage of pictures that showed his adult life. He was a military man, rode motorcycles, skied a lot, a real thrill seeker who worked hard and partied hard too. His beautiful, soft-spoken daughter told of her affection for him. She conveyed a few brief stories about his character and confirmed what I suspected about the guy. He appeared to be a lovable asshole. When his kids would crash water skiing, he would laugh hysterically until they swam back to the boat. She said, "I remember chopping wood in winter and thinking as a kid it was not what I wanted to be doing, but I look back at it now fondly."

Boy, could I relate to that. By the time I graduated high school, I considered myself a semi-professional landscaper.

I could hardly believe how eloquently she put his less desirable tendencies. She said, "When God's making his children, he puts in some good and throws in some bad. He likes to mix it up." I was thinking to myself, 'That has got to be the most polite way of calling somebody an asshole I've ever heard.' Let me tell you, that girl was really an awe-inspiring piece of work. She had me quite enamored. Apparently, the tough love worked.

The deceased being a well-liked guy, it came as no surprise the procession seemed a bit long, requiring four riders to handle all the cars. Even though the rain had let up, the roads were still wet and slippery. Visibility had improved though, the gray clouds made for a good line of sight without any bright sunlight or glare.

I WAS HOLDING an intersection as the cars of the procession went by in an orderly fashion. The last rider, Jackknife, came zooming by following the last car and it was time for me to go. Then I heard the sound: Locked up brakes, four car tires sliding on wet pavement, waiting to see how it would turn out. As always, your senses go into high gear and the time stretch begins. Didn't have to wait long. It turned out bad. It was a rear-ending with the violent sound of metal compressing that seems like an explosion. It sounded far worse than it really was, a fender bender but with some big time crunching, not just a slight damage hit, this one sounded serious. I was expecting more, like a chain reaction, but it was only those two cars, about thirty yards away.

Everyone in the car that got hit jumped out like it was some kind of Chinese fire drill, getting out from one car door to get back in another, but they weren't opening other car doors, just running around in hysteria. As soon as the mother shot out of the car she was literally jumping up and down in the intersection like a child having a tirade, screaming, "HELP ME!!!"

I had to make a decision. Here I am, standing in the middle of a major intersection and everyone thinks I'm a motorcycle cop. A serious accident happens a stone's throw away. Do I jump on the bike and take off to continue with the procession like I didn't see what just happened? -Leaving everyone in sight going *what the fuck*? Or do I try to get this sorted out a bit and catch up? It was a no-brainer for me. I wheeled the bike to the side of the road and told them to move the cars out of the way so we could see how bad the situation was or wasn't.

"My baby's hurt!" she screams. Thank God the other passenger in the mother's car was rational, because the driver had crossed over to the temporarily insane. I walked around to the back side of the car, expecting to see some horrible scene with the baby, judging from the mother's reaction, but all I see is an infant crying loudly, strapped in a baby seat in the back, just a little shook up like the rest of us. The kid's fine.

What bothered me was the mother running around like a chicken with its head cut off when her first concern should have been checking on or staying close to her infant, but instead chose to fly into hysterics, looking for someone, anyone or anything to blame.

The mother was so far gone, she couldn't even work her cell phone to dial 911. "My phone won't work!" she pleaded. She was so distraught that she was in another world completely. She gave me the cell phone and after turning it on and off a few times, I dialed 911 and gave it back to her. I figured maybe the emergency operator could calm her down. Nope. The rear end driver girl came out of her car with her license and insurance in hand and the mother tried to lay into her.

"She hit my baby!" she wailed.

Now, before anyone jumps to the defense of this young mother to make excuses for her, consider that the girl's first instinct was *not* to check on her child. No. It was to jump out of her car and make a scene and claim her victimhood. She screams her baby is hurt. It's not. She couldn't operate her own phone, she wanted to blame it. She's treating me like an indentured servant because she probably thinks her taxes pay my salary. They don't.

I scribbled down my name and phone number on the insurance envelope of the driver who caused the accident. My hands were so cold I could barely scrawl my own name and recognizable numbers.

"What's this?" she asked, snarling.

"If you need a witness or someone to clear up the details, this is my number."

Seeing as how crazy the girl in the rear-ended car was being, a level-headed witness with no stake in the situation might be useful I thought. The driver saw it strictly as a come on and was offended. Oooh, how I do not miss the snide attitudes of Portland girls.

By this time, the three other riders, a mile ahead by now, are wondering what had happened to me. I don't have a radio to tell them what's holding me up, or what's brought me down. Jack keeps waiting to see me in his mirrors as he holds the intersection. The last car comes by and I'm still nowhere in sight. He fears the worst and pulls up beside Hollywood, "Have you seen Mouse?"

"No," he says.

"He didn't pass me," Jack informs him. Jack calls over the radio to dispatch back at the office "I think Mouse might have witnessed an accident or been involved in one." Kickstand is the first person back at the office hearing this and is probably shitting bricks. The last time there was a call over the radios as a rider down, it was Kickstand. And worse yet, not only did he dump his bike in summer without his leather on, but his bike burst into flames with him pinned under it. A few skin grafts on his arms and he was back on the bikes in no time. But he of all people knew how fast things could go sideways.

HELP WAS on the way and it was time for me to go, so I told them I had to rejoin the procession I was a part of and took off. It took me two minutes to catch back up with the procession, through green lights, cutting in between traffic to get to the front of a line of twenty waiting cars. I caught up with Hollywood holding the last intersection. I pulled up next to him and explained how the woman was freaking out. He was in a bad mood already and said, "Not our responsibility."

And then it was back to the procession like nothing had happened. Powell Street was super hairy. We'd get to the intersection and there'd be ten cars waiting at the light. The rider would have to get the attention of cross traffic going two directions, stop them, then wave the waiting traffic through the red light so the hearse could keep moving. Riding in the narrow width between cars waiting in the left turn lane and those that want to go forward is an extremely delicate slow speed weave through dozens of cars and their external mirrors are like metal tree branches reaching out to knock you over.

Still cruising down the busy, congested Powell Street, I saw a Santa Claus fully decked out in costume and beard. I came screaming by him at 40 miles an hour with a thumbs up, yelling, "Santa Claus, my man!!" -having no idea how many times in the future I would don the same costume to humor kids and let them hang on to their belief in Santa just a little longer.

IT WAS A PRETTY weird and exhausting day for everyone. I was told that if I ever witnessed something like that again, it was my job to take off and let emergency services get there and sort it out, which didn't sit right with me, but hey, he's the boss. When we got back to the garage, referring to the distress call Jack made over the radio, Kickstand said to him with a smile, "Don't ever do that to me again. 'Bout gave me a heart attack."

Mentally processing what had happened back at that intersection, the whole thing still bothered me. From the first second to the last, the victim driver acted as if I were a public servant at her beck and call, able to order me around in any hysterical fashion she saw fit, no demand too great. Needless to say, I didn't care for her attitude, any of it. The irony is that the mother who stopped as directed and was paying attention got nailed for it by someone who wasn't being so observant. It bugged me that I had everybody shitting on me for trying to do the right thing, but I knew it would have bothered me even more if I'd just taken off and done nothing.

RIDE 82

A single ride on one of the most miserable weather days of the entire winter. Pouring rain followed by pounding drizzles. It stung my face riding through it and felt more like sleet than a downpour. I couldn't see a thing with my glasses on and stuffed them in a soaked pocket.

Doc and I left the garage, filled the tanks, and went to an Elmer's Pancake House down the street, where he said he had plans to meet up with someone he was quite keen on. We got a few looks as we came through the entrance in full gear, looking like we're there on official business or that we've been called about some incident, like some unruly customer demanding too much syrup, but hey, we need to eat like everybody else. In the corner there waited Doc's woman of great interest to him (which was putting it mildly), and four of her seven children. Don't even get me going about how mind-boggling it is to be a relatively young woman and already a mother of SEVEN, a single mother, looking to date. All that aside, she struck me as a really neat woman, and her two daughters were exceptionally kind. One of her daughters, about ten or twelve years old, won my heart in an instant. Having never seen me before, from the moment I sit down she's asking me if I'd like some coffee. She said she was buying and was holding two dollars in her hand.

Her offer was so kind and flattering I had to say 'No thanks.' I wanted to hit the road and get this ride over with, but the adorable daughter was persistent and kept asking if I was sure I didn't want a cup of coffee. It was a pretty good guess the girl had come by these two dollars from her mother, maybe as part of a plan to woo me over so I'd say good things to Doc about the situation. If so, it worked exactly as intended. By the time the waitress showed up with coffee in hand, the persuasive girl had swayed me to indulge in caffeine I didn't really want. I thanked her many a time. I asked them if they were out of school, and sure enough, they were on a two week vacation. Only problem was that she was grounded for a week for having a friend over at her house when her mom wasn't there.

I later told Doc to tell the woman that if I were governor of the state, I'd grant her daughter a pardon. That girl insisting to buy me a cup of coffee and taking such pleasure in it absolutely made my day.

 **RIDE 83**

I n the break room at the garage, four of us riders were hanging out shooting the shit before it was time to go. Typical conversation over paper dispenser cups of coffee, giving each other crap, the usual. We were just waiting on Hollywood to show up so we could all head out to the service together. He pulled up on his non-civilian cop bike, jumped off and took a few steps straight into the break room with a look of focused concern on his face. Right off the bat, he told us how Kickstand was no longer a person to be relied upon in any way whatsoever, whether it be about escort riding, limo runs, hearse drives, you name it. It seemed long overdue from all the stories I'd heard over the months, seemed like whenever there was a situation where something had gone wrong, he was somehow a part of it.

"It's just the five of us here from this point on," he said.

It's not like I was really in a position for this to have any effect on me, as in, being in a place to make a judgement call and do something differently as a result of it being with Kick-stand, but it was good to know that this particular person you're riding with should be treated like a rattlesnake in a corner. It was simply a heads up that anything to do with him was suspect and from here on out, his motives should always be questioned. Not given any details to go on, one could only imagine what had transpired to come to this conclusion and inform us, because it definitely wasn't a judgement he'd reached lightly. I had a hard time understanding how Meatball was included in this select five, but I felt kind of guilty for having acquired this respected trust and yet would be leaving the company in less than a week.

THE SERVICE WAS at that cool Franciscan-looking church down-town I'd become so familiar with, the one where my biological father lived around the corner at some flophouse above the bar. Jack came out of the main church door and I asked him if I had time enough to walk to the bar to see if my father was around. With some time to spare, I walked down to the bar in the full getup, went inside and started looking around. Every eye in that place was suddenly locked on me, the half awake hang dog faces of the dive bar regulars. My presence did seem to wake them up a bit, even if just for a moment. Dave was nowhere to be seen. I leaned toward the bartender girl who was looking me up and down.

With a mix of respect and hostility she said, "Can I help you?"

As politely as possible, I asked "Have you seen Dave Koester?"

Like many a bartender before her, she can't place a face to the name. She calls out to the early morning drinkers, "Dave Koester?"

A relatively young guy my age leaned away from the bar and said, "Haven't seen him yet today."

I thanked him and left, knowing that the first thing Dave would hear next time he walked in the bar, someone would say,

"Hey, Dave, there was a motorcycle cop in here looking for you yesterday."

And sure enough, I later heard he said, "Yeah, that's my son."

THE RIDE WAS easy and we got the procession to the cemetery no problem. With five guys, it should be a no-brainer without incident. From there, we riders split up, Doc and I heading back towards the garage while the other guys took off to go do another service. On the way back, Doc and I stopped at the liquor store down the street from my apartment, told him I wanted to get something real quick. Doc waited outside on the bike while I entered the place in full uniform for the first and only time I ever would. I can only imagine what must have been going through the minds of the staff: 'You gotta be shitting me, he's a cop?'

It was interesting how I was suddenly being treated with great respect and dignity by the customers and three employees, as if I had outed myself for what I really was. They had seen me so many times with such regularity, they could set their clocks by when I would arrive. Usually, I don't even have to tell them what I want it was so predictable, a fifth of McCormick's, a mid-level whiskey that wasn't too expensive, which I didn't get because of the price, but because it was smoother and didn't burn like the more expensive stuff. One time I went in there with a friend and to prove my point, I told him "Watch this."

Seeing me, the employee reached over for a fifth of my usual gut rot, rang it up, put it in a brown paper bag, I paid for it and walked out of there with a smile without having said a single word. This time, I bought a small bottle of some Irish whiskey for Hollywood for Christmas. He's got some Irish history, I can't remember what.

A few minutes later about a mile up the road, Doc and I were on 20th Street, behind ten cars waiting at a red light, sitting right outside my go-to video store where I would go to rent everything. It was a tiny little place, not a big Blockbuster or Hollywood video, with huge glass windows facing the street. Charlie, the girl in the video store who still thought I was a cop because I hadn't had the chance or need to dispel the impression, was on the phone in the window, talking on a landline to a customer. I saw her and waved; she waved right back. It was great. Little things like that make my day. Just that one sighting of me guaranteed her smiling face and kind personality for the duration of her employment there.

BACK AT THE GARAGE, I took the mini-bar sized bottle of whiskey and wrapped it in an orange funeral paper, but that wasn't enough to hide the fact it was a bottle. There were heaps of fresh cut flowers lying in a dumpster a few feet away. I stuffed the top of the wrapping paper with six different kinds of flowers, only two of which I thought I might have known the names of. Then, in what I thought was a stroke of pure genius, I wrapped the wire of a pink toe tag around the neck of the bottle. I crossed out the line that read, 'Deceased Name', and wrote in the blank, Hollywood. The line below read, 'Funeral Home'. I crossed out all the letters except the f-r-o-m, and wrote, M. Mouse. In the next lines I wrote, 'Happy Holidays! Thanks for the memories.' and left it on his desk.

ON THE WAY HOME, on my own motorcycle in street clothes, I was about five blocks from my apartment and I got ran off the road by a white van. It happened so quick I couldn't see the driver or get the license plate, it was all I could do to lock up the brakes, slide sideways on the wet pavement, then come to an abrupt crash into the sidewalk. If it weren't for my bike's crash bars sticking out around the engine, I surely would have broken my right ankle in nine different places and have steel pins to hold my bones in place.

I was just thankful I didn't go over the handlebars at that point. The bike died on me and wouldn't start for about half a minute. Felt like forever as I could see the van going through the light ahead, oblivious and without concern for what he'd done, driving around like he was inviting trouble and now he'd found some. I finally got it started again and took off after him (I think it was a him), passing cars one after the other on a slow two lane residential road, hell bent for that van. I knew there was a traffic light far up ahead, maybe about a mile, and if it was red, I could catch him there and get in his face, make a commotion. Do something. You just don't run me off the road, endanger my life, get a wave and a 'Have a nice day'. Actions have consequences. So I'm speeding up to the intersection, using all my skills and acquired confidence, I'm literally riding at the best ability of my life, but I have to pull way back and chill out because this intersection is a hairy one, you just don't go blowing through it even if the light is green in your favor, even in a car. You gotta make sure someone isn't barreling through it from the left or right despite your right of way. Lots of accidents happen here.

I get through the intersection, where the road climbs up to a much quieter part of town, all normal houses, should be easy to spot the van again and close in. Thing is, no white van. It got so far ahead of me and when it hit that free and clear area after the intersection, it must have really taken off because it was gone.

I was so screaming for blood I went riding around the area looking for that white van until I knew I wouldn't be able to find it. It was long gone. It's probably better I didn't catch up with him. Nothing good could have come from me going postal on a guy in a van who'd shown that rules and the constrictions of society don't apply to him. Road rage has unexpected consequences too. I guess I should have looked at the bright side. I nearly got killed by some asshole driver, but didn't. And tomorrow was Christmas.

Ice storm damage

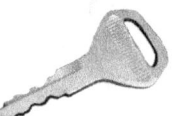 **RIDE 84**

O ver the Christmas holiday, Portland had been hit by a paralyzing ice storm, coating everything in sight with a heavy glassy-looking shell. Under the weight of the ice, trees that had withstood decades of rough weather now cracked and fell apart. The day after the storm, it was business as usual. I was scheduled to have a single ride with Hollywood that would be a milk run of only about two miles.

I took the cover off the bike outside my apartment and saw there was still a big chunk of sod from when I'd been run off the road by that white van and kicked it out of the crash bars. Not having been started after two days of freezing cold and rain, it didn't surprise me the beast wouldn't start. I had to push it down four hills to finally get it going, the family jewels taking a beating in the process. I managed to get to the office without any careless motorists trying to kill me with ignorance or inconsideration.

I'm ready to go at the garage, so I'm just hanging around in the break room waiting for Hollywood to show up. First thing he said when he walked into the garage was, "Thanks for the whiskey."

"You bet," I say.

He goes back to the shelf near the bikes, grabs a cardboard box and brings it to the break room.

"Is that what I think they are?" I ask.

"Better late than never," he says, opening a box of a kazillion orange funeral papers. We'd been out of them for a while now and it's surprising just how useful those little strips of paper are. Having those orange papers in hand seemed to make it easier to go up to people and ask them if they were heading to the cemetery or not. Made it easy to tell who had been approached or not, who was going and who wasn't, how big or how small your procession was really going to be. You tell every single one of them to turn on their lights and hazards, but most of the time, all they hear is lights. The hazards rarely got turned on without a reminder in the parking lot as we'd be getting ready to start rolling. On rainy days, which is the default setting in Oregon, just about everybody in the state drives with their lights on, sometimes making it difficult to recognize the last car in a procession if their hazards aren't blinking as well. You see a possible last car with its lights on like everybody else and no hazards, then catch a glimpse of an orange paper in the dashboard, and you know it's time to take off and get back up to the front.

Hollywood's bike is near empty and mine could use some topping off, so we head down to the Texaco station in no rush, we're doing fine on time. Hollywood fills his tank, hands me the pump and goes inside to pay because the credit cards haven't been working at their new, high-tech pumps lately. I fill my tank in no time, put the pump back, close my tank lid with the key and put it in the ignition. I reset the odometer and see the tank on the other bike could use closing. I put Hollywood's key in the lid, but it wouldn't turn the knobs to make it go back in the tank. Instead, the key bent like the cheap, thin piece of metal it was.

"Oh shit!" I said.

'O.K., don't panic', I thought, 'You've just bent Holly-wood's key to crap'. There must have been some special way to get the cap back in the tank with that tin foil key, but I didn't know what it was. I gently tried to bend it back in the other direction, but it didn't look good, still warped and like it wouldn't go back in the ignition. I tried ever so slowly to get it straight and then: Snap. The last centimeter tip came off in the lid and I knew I'd just created a world of shit.

Hollywood came out of the station ready to hit the road, thinking everything is o.k., and there I am saying, "Uh, we got a problem."

Just on sight, he can see this situation is totally Fubar. Hollywood says, "O.K., you ride this one and I'm gonna push you back to the shop with 5-7."

Me, Doc and Soda Pop had all seen this procedure once in our evals in the parking lot back in April. Hollywood put his front bumper on the back bar of Kickstand's bike, then hit the throttle, pushing it forward with enough force that Kickstand could compression start his bike. Both Hollywood and Kick-stand nearly went down in the process, their bikes wobbling wildly and almost dumping on the pavement, but managed to keep them up. It was an awesome sight. But that was just pushing Kickstand a few yards in an empty parking lot. Here he was saying he was going to push me on a dead bike a half mile back to the garage like that. And sure enough, he did.

He got on the only other bike available and fired it up. In the street, he cornered around, coming up on my left and said, "Alright, let's try this again," and we took off down the street.

At the service, waiting for it to wrap up, Hollywood and I had a lot of time to talk. I asked him about the difficulty they were having finding new escort riders as a result of six or so having moved on or retired since April. In response to the newspaper ad that initially caught my eye, there was even a 14 year old girl who had called, saying she had only ridden a dirt bike and didn't know exactly what the ad in the paper was about, just something about motorcycles. She was probably looking for her first job.

Hollywood told her something like, "Call back in ten years."

It never ceases to amaze me how many people they turn down and don't even ask them to fill out an application. Most of the ones they do have fill out the application have driving records four pages long.

Fortunately, all the drama of the day took place before the run and the ride itself was a piece of cake. I mean really, how much can go wrong in two miles? I'm coming home on my own bike in street clothes and stop in at the video store to rent the movie The Rock, but it's not there. This rental place is one of my regular haunts, have been going there for ages, for so long that I'd seen many employees come and go over the years, but only on one or two occasions did I go there in uniform. The cute girl, Charlie, who still thinks I'm a cop, says, "Just the person I was looking for. I've got a question. Do you know where I can get mace around here?"

This is back when mace was new and hard to come by. I was perplexed, mace being something I was never in the market for. I told her I wasn't sure, but I could sure find out.

 **RIDE 85 - 86**

I'm at a typical service and things are going well. There's no great tragedy being mourned and people are coming to terms with the loss of a loved one. It's how things go in the best of situations. The attendees start to make their way out of the building in the slow way they do at gatherings like this. I'm handing out the orange funeral papers as they pass by. A beautiful woman comes up to me holding her son in her arms and says, "Excuse me, but my son wanted to shake hands with the Power Ranger."

Ok, that's adorable. Kid thinks my cop getup makes me look like a sci-fi hero he sees on TV. I reached out to his tiny hand and shook it, saying something like, "Hey there, little guy, how are you?"

At that age, they're usually too shy to respond. However, he did notice a tiny little cut on my right index finger. He asked, "How did you get that owie?" quite perplexed.

He probably noticed because he thought that Power Rangers, just like cartoon characters, never really suffer permanent injuries, simply take a few hard knocks before obliterating their enemies with a sonic punch or something. I didn't really have a good answer for him when I thought about the cause, probably a sharp can or lid got me when I was opening it. The mother and I were having a great laugh about it all, so much so that I felt a twinge of guilt for being so happy at the funeral of a stranger, but it's little unexpected moments like that that really make your day, make up for all the other stuff that can happen.

The procession itself went great. Gravel, to combat the ice storm of two days ago, was everywhere in the streets and of special concern when we'd be jamming back up to the front around the cars. Gravel on the street is like the equivalent of having someone throw a bucket of marbles on the ground as you try to make it across the crosswalk on two feet. Having the whole procession change lanes on the highway was also a bitch. So many variables; bogies wanting to merge from onramps, others wanting to change lanes, go around or get off the highway. Keeping everyone together was one part exerting control over what you could and one part crossed fingers. A scary, then frustrating prospect, but we pulled it off without mishap or close call. If only all services and runs should go this smoothly.

We had two hours to kill until we needed to be at the next service, which again was located a few blocks from where my biological father lived. I went to the bar below his apartment and walked by the huge security guy outside the front door, no hassle, nothing. This place was such a dive bar of bowery bums and lowlifes, they had to employ a dude outside to keep the criminally insane from entering, and this was a decade before the opioid crisis. I had to wonder how many people were on their list of being 86'ed and how often the bouncer would be involved in some scene.

Inside, it takes about five seconds to see Dave's not there and that I've got the attention of everyone in the place without making a sound. His jeep's outside, so he's got to be at his place upstairs. I get a buck from my pocket, four quarters from the change machine and give him a call. It must have rang eight times before he picked up. He said I didn't wake him, but he didn't know it was 11:30 in the morning.

He came down to the street a few minutes later and first thing he noticed was that the security guy gave me a rare, impressed look that I didn't see or care about. It never ceases to amaze me how people react completely differently because of the cop getup. The only difference between when I go out on my own motorcycle and the cop uniform is the helmet and the badge, well, and the brown polyester pants. But the difference in public perception and how I get treated is immense.

In the cop helmet, badge and walkie-talkie, I get treated with instant respect, and much is assumed about me. Everybody seems to think I know kung fu and the use of special pressure points that will disable people with a minimum of effort, like a Vulcan nerve pinch. Were I to come in there in my normal clothes, the bouncer would barely perceive me as a threat. In the cop getup, leather, boots and all, he knows he could never take me out by himself.

The difference is the same with passers-by, people walking around. In the cop outfit, they assume that I'm conducting important police business, something of urgency. The simplest question gets their full attention. They ponder for absolute certainty in their answers. Disrespect is rare. The badge negates people's concerns about me, gives credence to the intimidating look, whereas without it, they see me coming and can't hide the fear in their faces, seeing me as threatening. They look at me as if to say, 'Omigod. Is he coming over here?' Basically, the intimidating look is justified with the badge and getup, because the intimidation is meant for the bad guys, not so much the public. The same look is not cool without the badge because they think they will be the victims of the violent or criminal potential they suspect me of.

Hanging out at the bar for a little while, the female

bartenders were bending over backwards for me, not that I was asking much of them, coming by to see if I needed this or that. Thing is, had I come into the same bar years earlier in the cop getup, back when the owner hired only drop dead babes to pour the beer, my Friday nights might not have been so boring or alone. The potential for flirtatious cracks about frisking, body searches, chains and leather were there on offer, and if I didn't make the comments, they would have. But that was back then. Those days were clearly long gone. Just my luck.

Dave was not the greatest conversationalist and every time we spoke it always seemed to end in frustration, so I tried to keep it short. Checking the time, I left him at the bar to ride down the street and buy a C.D. for my sister's birthday. I'd been at that music store many times before, but going there in the appearance of a cop is like walking around with a hall pass. If nothing else, you don't get the suspicious glance upon entering that you might be a shoplifter.

At the second service, Doc and I now had more time to hurry up and wait. With quarters still in my pocket, I called my mother from a pay phone and shot the breeze for a while. The service had been mentioned on the news and mom knew the deceased guy's name, having known of him. My dad even played college football with the guy back in the day. They all went to O.S.U. at the same time.

Telling my mom about the procession later in the day, hearing every street and turn as we went along, she could easily see it all in her mind, even beating me to the last couple streets. I had been down all those streets before, but could never see it in my head. I told her she'd be great at my job because I could never visualize it beforehand, whereas she could see it clear as day. Even though I had lead maybe two or three processions from that place to the highway before, I still had to ask what route we were going to take to get down there, despite it being only three blocks away. I mean, my memory for streets is garbage. It was a limitation I knew I wouldn't be able to overcome, like my incredible lack of ability at math. As much as I wish they did, those parts of my brain either don't work or don't exist. You could do a brain scan while I was engaged in these things, attempting to do math or navigate around town and the results would show no activity.

The ride itself was so easy and without mishap, I don't remember a thing about it. On the way back from that second run, starting from Lake Oswego, Doc and I were waiting at a red light on busy Macadam Street, lots of traffic moving around in all directions. I saw some young kids in the cab of a pickup truck right next to us, watching the world go by from the rear window. I waved to them and they waved back. I pointed my big, black leather winter glove at them and made as if I was shooting at them, only smiling. Pew pew, pew pew... The mother in the front passenger seat thought it nice and playful, but had I not been smiling, she might have thought I was some sick, demented jerk, telling her husband to get away from us.

Doc was suddenly acting squirrelly, winding out the throttle a few times, cranking it loudly, waiting for the light to change, and said something like "Check this out."

The instant that light turned green, he ripped the throttle and popped a wheelie about two feet up in the air, lunging that huge white faring right up off the pavement. It was actually the first time I'd seen a wheelie on one of those monsters; not the kind of bike I'd ever seen do that. He nailed that thing back down on the road at fifty miles an hour and the landing was a little squirrelly too. I laughed a hollering whoop and yelled out, "ALRIGHT!!! That is sensational!" We were laughing about it for the next couple minutes. I know one thing was for sure, those kids in the pickup next to us saw an awesome sight and they were probably telling their friends about it hours later. What the parents thought about it was anybody's guess.

It might have been from seeing that stunt and a certain lawless behavior to it, that the driver of a red Toyota Supra was playing tag with us all the way from Lake Oswego through Portland, and that's a pretty long way. The car kept hanging back in our blind spot, like drafting in the other lane, never passing, but enjoying our regal flirtation with the speed limit. The driver figured out early on that we weren't going to or couldn't pull him over, so he played it to the hilt, screaming up to 75 miles an hour behind us on the interstate. I suppose when he noticed we didn't give him any signs to cool it, he knew he was in the clear and enjoyed it, like chasing an ambulance.

I didn't say anything about it to anyone, but that wheelie Doc pulled in the street also kinda bugged me. It's one thing to do some minor stunt on your own bike, but to do it on a company bike, representing the police, and in public in the city, Ugh. That's just poor judgement. Can't tell you how many videos I've seen of guys supposedly showing off on a bike and crashing, destroying the bike, breaking bones, all kinds of bad things and it's just not worth it. These people need to be avoided because they drag others down with them with their foolishness, crashing into other people, destroying property, all kinds of consequences. In worst case scenarios, the last thought that runs through their minds is: 'Woooo, look at me! I'm so cool. I'm so cool... Woooooo! -Oh shit I'm dead.' And no more stunts for them. I always wonder: How cool are they now? Was it worth it?

So no wheelies for me. I was perfectly content with two wheels on the ground and good traction.

RIDE 87 - 89

I t was one of those nights I've become so used to, where I lay in bed with my eyes closed, despite the fact that I'm as awake as anybody who's had three cups of coffee in the last hour. I might as well do long division in my head for how alert and conscious I was. I had a long time to think about the double header I'd have with Meatball in the morning. Turns out Meatball did have a nickname, I'd just never heard of it up to that point, and for some reason of lore it was Gadget. I could only assume that gadget was a fork. There was the inherent dread of his attitude and riding 'style', basically being an incessant jerk at every turn and corner, along with the buckets of rain that had been pounding on my window all night, to keep me as awake as I was.

I had that feeling you get when you know something in your life is going to end, some chapter coming to a close; maybe a risky job, a tour of duty, or moving away from a dangerous area. You have that feeling of being 'short', like you've come all this way and survived this much, that now something is bound to happen, just before you get out. I just wanted to leave O.F.S. on good terms and without incident.

Sometimes I would open my eyes in the dark only to see a jet black void blocking my sight of the ceiling. This furry feline mass would suddenly dart away almost without a sound but a whoosh, only for the void to silently return sometime later. I couldn't help but think of it as some kind of animalistic omen or premonition of my cat trying to express its concern with the telepathic message 'Don't go or this will be the last time I see you'. When my alarm finally goes off at 6:45 a.m., it's still dark outside from the gloom that hangs over the town.

A couple hours later, Gadget and I are on our way out to the first service in Beaverton. We take an exit off the highway that puts us right in front of a Texaco station, thinking that topping off the tanks would be a good idea because we've got the time. We head in towards the station and I can see two of the employees standing out near the pumps, the one especially catching my eye is a long-haired redhead who's spotted us coming in from a quarter mile away. As we cruise in, she's smiling and saying things to the gas jockey guy next to her.

Gadget pulls up to his pump of choice as I circle around the lot slowly. I pull up next to him and the redhead goes inside for something. The station guy has a pierced lip and a small hoop in his eyebrow. I say to him, "I get off my bike and the cute chicks go for the door."

"What?" he says, and I repeat something to the same effect. He looks back to the window to his co-worker.

"Well, she's checkin' you out man."

And as a matter of fact, he was right, she was. One needs to understand, this is unusual for me and happens rarely. When Gadget gets done pumping his gas, he hands me the hose so I can top off my tank.

"And I'll just bet she's got some super-cutie, sexy name, doesn't she?" I asked.

"Well, Bobbi."

I knew it. A feisty-looking, approachable, long-haired

redhead who likes motorcycles, with a name like Bobbi. I could deal with that. This gas jock had suddenly become my wing-man. He waved and yelled to her inside, "Hey Bobbi! Come here! Check out these bikes." She knew it was a ruse but came out anyway. She came up with a smile and said, "You know it's illegal to pump your own gas in the State of Oregon."

But she was just setting up my way in, where I could say something fun in return, like, "Well, I guess you'll just have to arrest me."

But I blew it. I just laughed and waved my hand like Gimme A Break. Try and stop an Oregon biker from pumping their own gas, whatever the law may be.

You can never close on a brief first meeting like that, somehow exchange contact information or set something up; you have to come back and try to make it happen. I didn't really get a good chance to check her out, but noticed she had on a ton of makeup and in that realization, the potential with Bobbi went no further.

WE GET to the first service and the waiting begins. Rain was coming down pretty steady and there really wasn't anywhere to go to get out of it other than inside where the service was being held. It's worth pointing out that as an escort at a service, standing under an umbrella in a downpour, or any degree of rain, is not an option. You either had rain gear and stood out in it, or got out from under it for just a little while. Your leather getting soaked all the way through was the norm, not the exception. So, we stood in the rain for a while, then went inside and paced around because there was nowhere to sit.

While handing out the orange papers as the people were coming out of the church, one woman said to me, "Nice uniform."

I love it when someone manages to still have a sense of

humor in light of the circumstances, especially when you least expect it. This is the same church as the kid who saw me as a Power Ranger a few days before. Seems to be a lucky place with a good vibe. We were even going to the same cemetery as last time, and yet I couldn't exactly remember the entire route. Hell, I didn't know how we were getting the two miles to the highway again. Gadget told me that it was two streets; a right on Lombard and left on Hall.

We get the cars on the road and he holds the right turn onto Lombard and I cruise up to the front, leading the hearse for a while. I see the major intersection ahead, which must be Hall Boulevard. It looks familiar, I think this has got to be the turn, but the sign reads Allen Street. Split second confusion. Did Gadget tell me the wrong street? Someone has to secure this intersection whether we're going straight or left, so I stop the cross traffic, but have positioned myself in the wrong place for a left turn and Gadget barks at me, "You're blocking the hearse."

I don't recall what exactly the problem was, but we get it sorted out and the rest of the run was smooth, just had to be super careful about all the gravel between the lanes. One bad lane change and you'd be spitting that gravel out of your mouth from being face down in it.

The last car turns into the cemetery and we get off the road and call into the office over the walkie-talkies. Hollywood tells us that a funeral home had called in an unexpected cancellation and needs us to do the run for them. Actually, it was one of Jawbone's runs that had been cancelled, as he was spread too thin to pull it off, so we got it instead. The day had suddenly turned into a triple header.

It was a run consisting of only two traffic lights and would probably take us all of five minutes, maybe three miles at best. We must have waited for an hour for those five minutes, with absolutely nothing to do but stand around or pace. Talking to

Gadget to while away the time was not an option. Spent most of our time watching some builders putting sheets of plywood on to the roof of the house they were building. Every house crew I've ever seen always has a token mascot dog. Theirs was a black lab that stood somberly looking out the unfinished second story window for long stretches of time, probably thinking about the next occasion it would run free in a park, fetch a ball or chase a cat.

Suddenly a drop dead blonde in a miniskirt came walking out the door of the building where the service was being held. She was an unbelievable woman, something straight out of a Victoria's Secret catwalk. Imagine if J-Lo or Beyonce suddenly came walking out right in front of you, out of nowhere and without an entourage. It was all I could do not to stare at her outright and I wasn't the only one who noticed this stunning woman as we stood there in shock. I have little doubt, looking like she did, she was as used to our amazed respectful glances as she was breathing the air. She was clearly dressed to be noticed, and we noticed.

In contrast to the first run, I do believe this one was flawless, merely for the fact that there's almost nothing you can screw up on such a short, simple run like that. The only other one that's this easy is from St. Anthony's church to St. Anthony's cemetery in Tigard.

We headed back to the office but had only about ten minutes to get out of the rain. I threw my soaked leather gloves and cotton scarf in the dryer. The damn weather was unrelenting. It was saving its big punch for later in the day, knowing we'd be hitting the road again. Didn't take long to get drenched all over again on the ride out to the third service, held at a Greek Orthodox church I'd never been to. This was my first true insight to Greek American culture other than going to a restaurant and smashing plates and I loved what I saw. It wasn't the architecture or the trappings of the event, there were Greek babes *everywhere*. Every single one of these women was stylishly dressed all in black, like they'd walked out of a Bond movie and showed up to this funeral as set decoration, eye candy extras walking around trying to distract you from what was really going on. Sexiest funeral I'd ever seen; stunners going this way and that, sitting around, drinking, laughing. It's like the host of a fashion show was doing live commentary in my head:

"Oh and what's this? Making her way across the room we have Lady Papadakis, whom having just turned 50 this last month, is showing she still has what it takes to compete with the 20 and 30 somethings with their youthful curves and energy. She's wearing a custom fitted Pierrotucci Italian leather skirt with matching Louboutin heels. And just look at those things, four inches long and she walks in them like she was born with them on her feet, strutting about with the grace of a gazelle. Looks like those yoga classes and Mediterranean diet are really keeping her in top form."

And the whole thing felt very festive, not a downer but almost like a wedding, when a person passes in a timely fashion at the end of a richly full life. At the end of the service, everyone in attendance lined the path to the hearse, where everybody had a part in carrying the casket at one point or another, passing it along until they closed the back door of the car. Then they all went next door to have a shot of whiskey and coffee. Interesting traditions I thought. I could watch this all day, it was fascinating. I thought it was a helluva lot better than some of the scenes I'd witnessed at other services, like mourners seemingly possessed by wailing demons whose screams had the hair on the back of your neck standing straight up. Total contrast. One seems like a pleasant acceptance of the ebb and flow of life and death, while the other seems more like performance art.

As the service went on and the day grew later, Gadget grew more and more concerned that he'd have to leave before the run got underway so he could take his son to his Tae-Kwon-Do class. This wasn't the first time Gadget had done this, thrown a bone in the works and made somebody cover for him for the same reason. It was kinda hard to believe Hollywood would put up with that, but I knew he was pretty shorthanded at the time. While Gadget's availability was shaky at best, I could hardly get one day off a week to look for another job.

Gadget calls Hollywood at the office and asks for someone to cover for him, so he sends out Doc, who had just returned from a 200 mile odyssey to Salem and back. Just when Doc is thinking he's going to get out of the weather, they send him out on one last, rain-soaked run before sundown. Turns out that Doc was actually looking forward to this one because his dad was in attendance and the deceased was a good family friend. It gives you an idea of just how long the service went on, the fact that it would have made Gadget late to do his personal stuff, call the office and get Doc on his way out there, and there was still time to spare.

Gadget takes off and Doc arrives in no time afterwards and as soon as he parks his bike, he goes inside to look for his dad, but missed him only by minutes. He mingles with people he hasn't seen in quite a while, probably having never seen him in this cop getup before. I stay outside, not knowing anyone of course, and if I go in there everyone will know I'm standing around just so I can steal glances of the beautiful women.

Doc calls me inside for a shot of whiskey with a coffee chaser.

"It's tradition," he says.

'Not mine.' I'm thinking. 'What? Are you crazy? A shot before a run?' I figure Hollywood would have our assess if he found out and what must the family members be thinking? - Two cops having shots of whiskey before taking grandpa to the cemetery, but Doc insisted. We toasted the shot glasses and slammed the whiskey. My concern was that any fuck ups in the run, big or small, would be associated with that one shot.

Doc and I agreed the route would consist of only three streets. Just a few roads, but a million cars to weave through to get to the destination. We'd go up Glisan to 92nd, take a right, then take a left at Powell up to the cemetery in the next town. The family connection ever-important in his mind, he says that of all the runs, he really wants to get this one perfectly. Of course, so do I. This shit's downright dangerous in these kinds of conditions.

We get under way. Doc is up the street holding the first light while I'm making sure no one from the neighborhood doing their business gets into the procession. Once you hit the road, it's like starting a clock, like you see in modern movies of holding up a bank. Seconds count. You're holding up traffic, things can go wrong, things change on a dime, the longer you and cars in the procession are exposed, the more you're in harm's way. The cars from the service kept coming, stopping to ask me which way to go. One car turns and joins the others, the next car goes the other way and on their way home, making huge gaps in the procession and taking a painfully long time. I could tell on that first turn that this run was going to be a real bitch.

It was raining way too hard to be wearing glasses of any kind. I couldn't read the street signs through the sheet of water over my specs. Now riding down the first road, I was leading the hearse and had to skillfully take off my glasses, get my front pocket unzipped and get those stubborn fuckers in there. It wasn't easy, especially as I was slowing down in first gear. This took what felt like forever in fidgeting, trying to get them to where they needed to be in my sopping wet clothes.

By the time I got them in the pocket, I knew we were getting close to 92nd. Now everything was a blur for a different reason, not the rain, just no focus. I squinted to read the street signs that were too far away. 90th, 91st, had to be that next one. When I jammed up ahead and held the right turn onto 92nd, I knew something was wrong. It was a little side street that looked like it went nowhere and that's exactly what it was.

I'd held the turn so the hearse could have gone straight past me if this wasn't what we wanted. The driver took the right turn anyway and lead the twentysome cars into a residential neighborhood. Doc about flipped. He was yelling, "No! This is NOT what we wanted!"

He said words to that effect a few times and when I asked him about the directions I'd quoted him on, he said, "There's 92nd Street, 92nd Court, 92nd Way, and we wanted 92nd Way."

I'd chosen the first 92nd we came to that I could see.

I wasn't going to argue about it. I did exactly what I was told, even though it didn't seem to make sense.

The easiest way out of the situation was blocked by a huge pile of fallen tree branches from the ice storm half a week ago. Doc turned the hearse around and we lead the procession back out onto Glisan, took the right turn at 102nd. He said that he'd told the coach driver at the last minute we were going to go right at 102nd instead. Through this admission, Doc was basically saying, 'Guess I should have told you too.'

The sense of danger and urgency seemed to be increasing with each intersection. Things were only getting more complicated. Oregon was in a state of emergency, some parts recovering from the ice storm, mudslides and flooding, while others were still getting the brunt of it as this was unfolding. Portland had turned into the Land of Ten Million Lakes. Drainages were clogged with debris, creating small oceans, barricaded off with signs stating the obvious: High Water. We were forced to go through the shallow parts of pool-sized puddles, a foot deep. The engines hiss loudly as they touch the water and huge clouds of steam rise up like the bikes have exploded in smoke, quickly dissipating in the air.

Then came the mother of all crossroads. I was the lead bike coming to a four way intersection, two lanes and a left turn lane in every direction. And that cross traffic was really moving. To further complicate things, there were commuter train tracks going through the intersection under the path of the procession. The hearse pulls up behind a few cars waiting at the red light. I get to the front and stop the oncoming traffic to the left, then get the attention of the cross traffic to the right and they stop, so we're good to go.

I wave the waiting cars that aren't part of the procession to go through the red light and get everyone out of the way. I'm off the bike at this point, having got everybody's attention, with the exception of one car, like a stray asteroid barreling towards Earth to wipe out the dinosaurs. The first car of the procession is a tiny little sportscar like a Mazda Miata and the driver hesitantly follows my instructions, going through the red light into the intersection. Like a hell bent tank, out of sight comes a beefy Multnomah County work truck, screaming through the intersection at full speed, missing the tiny sportscar by a car length. Am sure the driver of that lead car saw his life flash before his eyes, that feeling you have when you know everything would have turned out badly, the worst, if things had unfolded only a moment sooner. It was a *real* close call, the closest. Had that car started forward one second earlier and not been so reluctant, there would have been at least one fatality, if not two.

Imagine it from the driver's point of view of that Multnomah County truck. He's screaming down the road, pressed for time to get something done, the light up ahead is green in his favor, but for some reason, cars in the other lanes aren't going forward and he doesn't know why. He can't really see what's going on in the intersection he's fast approaching. Probably figures they're not paying attention. Oh well, let's just blow right by them... and by the time he clears the traffic blocking his view, and now sees the police bike in the middle of the intersection, he's flying through it and doesn't have time to even touch the brake before he's T-boning a matchbox car at the head of a funeral procession.

We all shared the same thought: Holy shit, that was close. Having missed the car by inches, the truck kept hurtling along and was quickly out of sight.

I pulled the bike forward to better secure that part of the intersection and see any potential cars not paying attention like what had just happened. I waved the first car through once more and thankfully he cleared the intersection. The whole procession started forward once more, the great crisis narrowly averted and I shit you not, just as the hearse was going over the tracks, a MAX commuter train comes barreling at it from around the corner. All the intersection lights automatically switch to red so all the traffic will stop and the train can go through, yet here are all these cars, bumper to bumper, sitting on the tracks. It was really bad. The hearse was able to get out of the way in time and I stopped the car behind it, but that MAX driver did some serious braking to avoid an accident. It was a mess. Once the cars were out of the way, we could get the MAX train heading down the line and things back to normal, as if anything about this day was normal. Once we got the cars through that intersection, I knew we were free and clear. I can't remember a set of near misses that bad before, where two cars would have creamed each other like an atom smasher and a train nearly crunched those who couldn't get out of the way.

.   .   .

WHEN WE REACHED THE CEMETERY, Doc parked his bike up the hill with all the cars in the procession, like family. I parked my bike down the hill. To park where Doc had, you had to go up a soggy gravel road that had a flash flood mini river carved out of it, gushing brown, muddy water. He stood outside the circle of close family around the casket. I walked up the hill and watched the service from a respectable distance. I didn't want to go back to the office without him. Didn't want to be a dickhead. I wondered what the family might think if I just took off. It probably would have made no difference to him or the family. They would understand someone wanting to get out of the cold rain as soon as possible, but sticking around just seemed like the right thing to do. In all those runs before, this was the first time I'd seen this part of the service. We always head off when the last car turns into the cemetery, not stick around and observe. After the whole event came to an end and he said his goodbyes, Doc and I rode back to the garage with a sense of relief. Despite the horrible weather, long hauls and dangerous conditions, we'd got through another day of this sometimes punishing and perilous job.

I didn't know it at the time, but that would be my last run. I wasn't thinking of it that way while I was doing it. I might have been scheduled for one the next day, so I wasn't sure. There was no reason to think this would be it, but it was. Tomorrow was New Year's Eve and it would be the last day I'd be available for them. Only fitting that my last day would be another trial by water, as usual. On a bike every day in Oregon, rain is your constant nemesis and those kind of downpour runs are the ones that challenge you the most. Too bad that final run couldn't have been closer to perfect on my part, have been a better demonstration of my riding ability and how far I'd come in those eight months. I asked back at the office if I was scheduled for the next day and when they told me I wasn't, I was relieved. I was off the hook. No more close calls in bad conditions. Cold, wet and miserable for not enough money to pay the rent. It was the coldest time of year and I was caught up in all the worst aspects of winter riding, thoroughly tired of them. Had I left the company on a sunny spring day, I might have had a different outlook; had misgivings about leaving and think of all the fun I'd be missing.

There weren't any sentimental goodbyes or movie-ending sendoffs, no pats on the back or solemn handshakes; I would be making my exit from a chapter of my life in a way that didn't call attention to myself, my work being done and for whatever reason, time to move on. It's a pattern I would repeat often over the years, seeming to exit through a side door without fanfare or notice, like slipping out the back.

I thought of the things I would remember most about my time there. I would never forget the sound of the engine, *that* particular engine, and how it winds through second and third gears with purpose, like it's hungry for speed, gets to fourth where you're cruising smoothly, then put it into fifth when you were really screaming. And that sense of rush, the speed, coming from the back of the line after the last car passes, charging right into traffic barreling at you in the same lane. You've been given permission to do this crazy stuff, ride around like the rules of the road don't apply to you, within reason, but in the act of doing something good. I can see why cops of all stripes, state, county and local, would rather do this than sit at home in their time off. I know none of them were doing it for the money. Who in the right mind would? But you get lulled in and hooked on it, a ring you don't want to part with, a calling you answered. And there was a little voice in the back of your head, reminding you that you had been chosen to do this, to the exclusion of many others, yet we all have to let go of it at some time. All of us had to move on when it wasn't working out any more so we could go Frodo some other mountain.

Doc asked me if I was going to clean out my locker that

day and I said no because I thought it would be a hassle best left for another time. Turns out it took three minutes and the only thing I left behind was a big round stereo magnet, stuck inside the locker. Right then and there the job ended, we all went our separate ways, which back then, was instantly, long before ubiquitous social media and easily keeping connections like that. Overall, it was a great experience while it lasted. I got out while I was ahead. Not only was it a blast, but it gave me a window into what it would be like to literally be someone else with a different career, how I would be perceived by the public, how people would treat me in a way that was previously unknown. Kind of like a relationship you wish you could save, it's hard to walk away from a situation where you're wanted and appreciated in search of something more. That something more was strictly financial. As I have thought to myself and told people over the years, if that job had paid a livable wage, I would have never left.

O.F.S. as a company is now long gone, the company having gone under, out of business for whatever reasons, who knows? I could find out, but don't want to know. I want to remember it the way it was and not think about its demise or downfall. I did an internet search to see if there's anything like it to take its place and sure enough, there is. I see now that a new company uses compact, lighter bikes that are so small they look like scooters, yet are 1300cc's of what must be raw screaming power. The requirements for getting hired are now much more stringent than in my day, needing much more riding experience and a squeaky clean lifestyle. Amazing how they can still be so discerning in their new hires when the job is such a time drain and has zero financial incentive. Some things about the job remain unchanged. It's still a virtually volunteer-like position with wages that are basically beer money. But as the website says, you'll have memories that will last a lifetime, and I do.

Doc and I waiting, taken by Jackknife with my camera

IMAGE DETAILS

Chapter Headings

Chapter 1 - My 500cc Yamaha Virago, otherwise known as a piece of junk. After seeing some video I shot, Hollywood told me it sounded like a lawnmower. It did.

Chapter 2 - My State of Oregon badge.

Chapters 3, 5, 10, 12, 29, 33, 36, 51 & 57 - A model of a Kawasaki KZ1000 I made over the course of 5 weeks in Osaka.

Chapter 4 - My whistle, The Acme Thunderer.

Chapter 6 - My tombstone mug that I drew the decal for in the break room of a marketing research company I worked for back in 1993. Only two of these mugs exist and I gave the other one away.

Chapter 13 - The exact kind of orange funeral papers we used.

Chapter 15 - Old 90's Harley police bike provided by Francis Deposito.

Chapter 17 - Mighty Mouse image designed by Paul Elliot .

Chapter 20 - The badge on my uniform shirt.

Chapter 22 - Image of red bandana provided by Urban Classics - TB Int.

Chapter 23 - Sign provided by SmartSigns.

Chapter 27 - Buffet for funeral service provided by Zest4Events.com and Foyetography in London.

Chapter 28 - A shot I took of the Monte Carlo on a rainy night, years before it burned to the ground in 2002.

Chapter 30 - My banged up Pentax K1000 film camera, held together with three kinds of tape in the end, which was the only camera I had from high school in 1984, to well into my time in Japan when digital cameras became affordable and commonplace, retired around 2006. It was used for all the motorcycle escort pictures as well as cemetery pictures seen on the photo pages, with the exception of Japanese cemeteries, which were digital.

Chapter 34 - Hearse image courtesy of Motorland Classic Cars, Arundel, Maine.

Chapter 41 - Piedmont Cemetery in Oakland, where it all started. Taken on a road trip from Southern California to Portland during my student days, around 1988.

Chapter 42 - The St. John's Bridge, courtesy of iStockphoto.com.

Chapter 46 - My first full face helmet.

Chapter 47 - An old green hearse for sale on eBay, courtesy of Brett @ bocollect.

Chapter 55 - Toe tag image courtesy of SmartSigns.

Chapter 56 - An actual key of a KZ1000, thin and flimsy.

Image Gallery

Page 1
   Top - One of my favorite tombstone images, from a Los Angeles area cemetery.
   Bottom - Lone Fir Cemetery, Portland, Oregon. Got this one published as a full page spread in Camera and Darkroom Magazine, which was one of the best photo magazines of its day. That's snow on the left shoulder of the female carving, which is why I called it The Cold Shoulder. I was told that the reason the carving in stone looks so odd is because back then they would be carved from a picture or painting.

Page 2
   Top - Lone Fir Cemetery, Portland, Oregon. A family crypt which was later used in the film Body of Evidence with Madonna and Willem DaFoe.
   Bottom - Piedmont Cemetery, Oakland, California, 1987. From the first shots I took of that cemetery while in art school.

Page 3
   Top - Close up of a tombstone from the 1850's of a

drowning victim with the empty boat, the waves and hands in the water. Lone Fir Cemetery, Portland, around 1996.

Bottom - Formerly known as Hollywood Cemetery, this image always makes me think of Prometheus getting his liver ripped out day after day.

Page 4

Top - Calistoga, California, around 1990. A cemetery off the side of the road on one of my trips back home to Oregon from Southern California.

Bottom - Same Calistoga cemetery, same day.

Page 5

Top - Lone Fir Cemetery mid 1990s. One of the last two pictures taken on a roll of Tri-X film. Having dropped acid about an hour before this shot, no one believed me about the rabbits until I developed the film.

Bottom - Family crypt in Lone Fir Cemetery.

Page 6

Top - Piedmont Cemetery, Oakland, California, 1988. Had to use a Cokin filter to get that color.

Bottom - Piedmont Cemetery as well from the late 80's.

Page 7

Top - Kyoto, Japan, around 2010.

Bottom - Cemetery in Inuyama, Japan, where I lived for around 5 years.

My Harley in Japan with Inuyama Castle in the background, 2010.

ACKNOWLEDGMENTS

To my Parents, who supported me through the toughest of times, having no idea anything would ever come of this.

Hollywood - A million thanks to one of the best bosses and most understanding people. Thanks for hiring me, despite myself.

Debbie Irwin - Voice talent and coach who took such an interest in this chapter of my life, I felt compelled to finish the story and get it off the backburner after 25 years.

Christine Veronica Morse - My immense appreciation for the support, encouragement and red pen better than any other.

Kohel Haver - For great legal advice and keeping me out of trouble.